DERSHOWITZ ON KILLING

Also by Alan Dershowitz

The Price of Principle

The Case for Vaccine Mandates

The Case for Color-Blind Equality in an Age of Identity Politics

The Case Against the New Censorship: Protecting Free Speech from Big Tech, Progressives, and Universities

Cancel Culture: The Latest Attack on Free Speech and Due Process

The Case for Liberalism in an Age of Extremism: or, Why I Left the Left But Can't Join the Right

Confirming Justice—Or Injustice?: A Guide to Judging RGB's Successor

Defending the Constitution

Guilt by Accusation: The Challenge of Proving Innocence in the Age of #MeToo

Defending Israel: The Story of My Relationship with My Most Challenging Client

The Case Against Impeaching Trump

The Case Against BDS: Why Singling Out Israel for Boycott Is Anti-Semitic and Anti-Peace

Trumped Up: How Criminalization of Political Differences Endangers Democracy

Electile Dysfunction: A Guide for Unaroused Voters

The Case Against the Iran Deal

Terror Tunnels: The Case for Israel's Just War Against Hamas

Abraham: The World's First (But Certainly Not Last) Jewish Lawyer

Taking the Stand: My Life in the Law

The Trials of Zion

The Case for Moral Clarity: Israel, Hamas and Gaza

The Case Against Israel's Enemies: Exposing Jimmy Carter and Others Who Stand in the Way of Peace

Is There a Right to Remain Silent? Coercive Interrogation and the Fifth Amendment After 9/11

Finding Jefferson: A Lost Letter, a Remarkable Discovery and the First Amendment in the Age of Terrorism

Blasphemy: How the Religious Right is Hijacking Our Declaration of Independence

Pre-emption: A Knife That Cuts Both Ways

Rights From Wrongs: A Secular Theory of the Origins of Rights

America on Trial: Inside the Legal Battles That Transformed Our Nation

The Case for Peace: How the Arab-Israeli Conflict Can Be Resolved

The Case for Israel

America Declares Independence

Why Terrorism Works: Understanding the Threat, Responding to the Challenge

Shouting Fire: Civil Liberties in a Turbulent Age

Letters to a Young Lawyer

Supreme Injustice: How the High Court Hijacked Election 2000

Genesis of Justice: Ten Stories of Biblical Injustice that Led to the Ten Commandments and Modern Law

Just Revenge

Sexual McCarthyism: Clinton, Starr, and the Emerging Constitutional Crisis

The Vanishing American Jew: In Search of Jewish Identity for the Next Century

Reasonable Doubts: The Criminal Justice System and the O.J. Simpson Case

The Abuse Excuse: And Other Cop-Outs, Stories and Evasions of Responsibility

The Advocate's Devil

Contrary to Popular Opinion

Chutzpah

Taking Liberties: A Decade of Hard Cases, Bad Laws, and Bum Raps

Reversal of Fortune: Inside the Von Bülow Case

The Best Defense

Fair and Certain Punishment: Report of the 20th Century Fund Task Force on Criminal Sentencing

Courts of Terror: Soviet Criminal Justice and Jewish Emigration (coauthored with Telford Taylor)

Criminal Law: Theory and Process (with Joseph Goldstein and Richard Schwartz)

Psychoanalysis, Psychiatry, and Law (with Joseph Goldstein and Jay Katz)

DERSHOWITZ ON KILLING

HOW THE LAW DECIDES WHO SHALL LIVE AND WHO SHALL DIE

ALAN M. DERSHOWITZ

HOT BOOKS

Hot Books may be purchased in bulk at special discounts for sales promotion, corporate gifts, fund-raising, or educational purposes. Special editions can also be created to specifications. For details, contact the Special Sales Department, Skyhorse Publishing, 307 West 36th Street, 11th Floor, New York, NY 10018 or info@skyhorsepublishing.com

Hot Books® and Skyhorse Publishing® are registered trademarks of Skyhorse Publishing, Inc.®, a Delaware corporation.

Visit our website at www.skyhorsepublishing.com.

10 9 8 7 6 5 4 3 2 1

Library of Congress Cataloging-in-Publication Data is available on file.

ISBN: 978-1-5107-7571-8
eBook: 978-1-5107-7572-5

Cover design by Brian Peterson

Printed in the United States of America

Acknowledgments

Thanks to Maura Kelly for typing the manuscript, to Tony Lyons and Hector Carosso for turning it into a finished product, and to my wife, Carolyn Cohen, for her continuing love and inspiration.

Dedication

This book is dedicated to my first law professor (fall of 1959), Guido Calebresi, who inspired me to think and write about tragic choices in law and life.

Contents

The Relationship between Death and Life

———

Death dominates the news. Ukraine, mass shootings, killings of minorities, the death penalty, assassinations, terrorism, the COVID virus, natural disasters, suicides, spousal killings, and much more. The right of a pregnant woman to abort a fetus also stimulates debates about death because women will die if not allowed to have life-saving abortions, which—according to pro-life advocates— require the "killing" of fetuses.

Death has always dominated history, from the time Cain killed Abel and Abraham was commanded to kill Isaac. Much of Greek mythology revolves around killing. The epochs of humankind are filled with accounts of the death of humans at the hands of other humans.

The great scholar Steven Pinker has brilliantly documented that violent deaths from warfare, crime, executions, and other forms of predation have actually diminished over the centuries, as have deaths from illness and natural disasters. But it sure doesn't seem that way now, perhaps because the media pervasively, if not selectively, reports on what appears to be a pandemic—both medical and bellig- erent—of death.

It is true that as a species we live longer than ever before, espe- cially in some parts of the globe. In these places, the ratio between deaths and births at any given time has decreased over the centuries, despite lower birth rates in many areas. There is, of course, a direct correlation between birth and death rates, because all people who are born eventually die, some sooner than later. There are now more people alive on our planet than at any time in history, despite lower birth rates, because survival rates are much higher in most parts of the world. All of us now living will die. So, there will be more deaths than ever before. Death will become an even more pervasive aspect of life.

Historically, the younger that people die, the higher the birth rates under most circumstances. When families need children to help support them, they tend to have more of them, if some die in childbirth or during the early years. In some cultures and religions, high birth rates persist, even in the absence of early death rates. During usual times (I resist the word "normal"), there is generally some direct relationship between early death and higher birth rates. This changes, of course, during wars, famines, or other phenomena that cause both early death and lower birth rates.

Death has always been with us, both physically and emotionally, regardless of external contributing factors. The knowledge Adam and Eve received from eating the forbidden fruit was that they were going to die.[1] Only humans know they are mortal. As Kafka put it, "The meaning of life is that it ends": we are all doomed to die, and we know it. Many mortals refuse to accept the inevitability of death—of an end to being. Hence, the promise of heaven and the threat of hell. But even for those who believe in some kind of after-life, death is the permanent ending of corporeal life as we know it here on Earth.

Is Death Different?

"Death is different," as judges and legal scholars have observed in distinguishing capital punishment from imprisonment. Justice Scalia

---

1   See Alan Dershowitz, *Genesis of Justice: Ten Stories of Biblical Injustice that Led to the Ten Commandments and Modern Morality and Law* (New York: Grand Central Publishing, 2000).

wondered whether that was so, in light of his certain belief in an afterlife. To him, death was "no big deal." Here is how he put it:

> Indeed, it seems to me that the more Christian a country is the less likely it is to regard the death penalty as immoral. Abolition has taken its firmest hold on post-Christian Europe and has least support in the church-going United States. I attribute that to the fact that, for the believing Christian, death is <u>no big deal</u>. Intentionally killing an innocent person is a big deal: it is a grave sin, which causes one to lose his soul. But losing this life, in exchange for the next? The Christian attitude is reflected in the words Robert Bolt's play has Thomas More saying to the headsman: "Friend, be not afraid of your office. You send me to God." And when Cranmer asks whether he is sure of that, More replies, "He will not refuse one who is so blithe to go to Him." For the nonbeliever, on the other hand, to deprive a man of his life is to end his existence. What a horrible act! [emphasis added]

Scalia is certainly the exception, even among believers, most of whom regard death as a very "big deal," even if it sends them to God.

To me, death, especially if inflicted by the state, has always been a big deal. My own legal career as a criminal defense lawyer has been deeply involved with death-and-life decisions. I have represented numerous defendants who have been charged and convicted of murder, attempted murder, assault with attempt to kill, conspiracy to kill, and other forms of homicide. I have defended death penalty cases as well as those involving long terms of imprisonment. Fortunately for my clients, I have won the overwhelming majority of my death-and-life cases, thus saving some from the death penalty and others from long imprisonment. I still have several homicide cases pending, because I never give up until my client is either freed or dies. Some of my clients have been guilty; some innocent; and some guilty of lesser crimes but not guilty of the charged homicide. None to my knowledge has ever hurt anyone after they were freed. I have turned down several homicide cases but never based on the seriousness of the accusation alone, since even those accused of the most heinous of crimes should be zealously represented. Many of these cases involved indigent defendants who could not pay a fee.

Death, Life, Culture, and Religion

My connection to death and life has also been manifested in my passion for culture. Much of the world's great art—novels, plays, poetry, opera, paintings, sculpture, music, religious writings—is about death, as Kafka reminded us. Art is about life, and the narrative of life is incomplete without death. Comedy—gallows humor—is often about death. As Woody Allen put it: "I'm not afraid of death. I just don't want to be there when it happens." Even the ignorant sports metaphor "It ain't over till the fat lady sings" is really about death, since the fat lady sings <u>throughout</u> the entire opera; it's over only when she <u>dies</u>!

I have written two novels and an opera libretto about death. The first novel (*Just Revenge*) and the libretto (*Hinnini*) are centered around the Holocaust, the other novel around the Mideast conflict. Death has also figured in several of my nonfiction books, hundreds of my op-eds, and many of my classes. I am reluctant to declare myself an expert on matters of death, but I certainly have long been interested in that grim subject. It will only increase as I get closer to the reaper!

In the Bible, God says: "I have set before you life and death." He then commands, "Choose life." Most do, when they have that choice. But not all do, and even when they do, it is sometimes appropriate to choose death, if a value more important than one's own life is at stake. To become a martyr is to choose death over life, as many have done through history and even now. The human experience includes tragic choices, or choices of evils, the most important of which often involve choosing death over life.

These tragic choices are generally regulated, at least to some extent, by the state, and thus by the law. Though they cannot control all life-or-death decisions, governments do often determine who shall live and who shall die: in declaring wars, ordering executions, authorizing the use of deadly force, permitting or denying abortion, providing or mandating vaccines, controlling climate change, allowing or refusing asylum for endangered migrants, and other life-and-death rulings.

Those who believe that all choices are ultimately made by God pray for life, as in the central prayer on Yom Kippur, the holiest day in the Jewish religion:

> On Rosh Hashanah will be inscribed, and on Yom Kippur will be sealed: how many will pass from the earth and how many will be created; who will live and who will die; who will die at his predestined time and who before his time; who by water and who by fire, who by sword, who by beast, who by famine, who by thirst, who by storm, who by plague, who by strangulation, and who by stoning.

When I recited this awesome prayer as a child growing up in Brooklyn during the 1950s, I could not imagine anyone dying by plague, famine, sword, strangulation, stoning, or beast. The Holocaust was fresh in the Jewish collective memory, with survivors all around us, but the esoteric causes of death listed in the ancient prayer were a distant aberration. What we feared, mostly for our parents and grandparents, were heart attacks, strokes, cancer, and being run over by a car or truck (as I was at three years of age). Every morning, upon awakening, we recited another scary prayer about death, warning "that if one of [the many body orifices] were ruptured, or if one of them were blocked, it would be impossible to exist. . . ." That I could worry about!

The fear of death was a salient part of our young lives, especially in the shadow of the Holocaust. My first conscious contact with death was during the post-World War II era, when survivors of death and concentration camps came to our neighborhoods and schools, some bearing the tattoos of death and near death. We rarely discussed what had happened to them and their families, many of whom did not survive. But at a visceral level, we knew that death was all around us. Then one of our neighbor's sons—who was several years ahead of us in our local Yeshiva—was killed fighting for Israel's independence. That made death even more immediate and salient. There but for the grace of God, and a few years of age and location, go we!

Death remains salient at every age, though with differing priorities. As Phillip Roth observed, near the end of his life: "Growing old is not a battle. It is a massacre." Yet, for most people, growing old is better than the alternative. Those of us who are fortunate enough to experience old age, even with its slings and arrows, understand this, even as we complain about the pain. As an aging friend once observed: "At our age, if you have no pain in the morning, you're probably dead."

We cannot end death. Nor can we even reduce certain of its causes. But there are many that can be impacted by human interventions. As I write these words, there is good news about certain kinds of cancers seeming to be amenable to new therapies. Medical innovations have saved many lives and will continue to do so. Many deaths are directly caused by human interventions, such as Russia's attack on Ukraine and other wars and warlike acts, terrorism, mass shootings. Some are caused by human unwillingness to intervene, such as the refusal by many to be vaccinated against deadly diseases. Others involve tragic choices, such as whether to allow a pregnant woman to obtain a late-term abortion to reduce her risk of death. Some such as unjustified police shootings can be curtailed by better training. Others by imprisoning violent predators. Still others by expanding opportunities for troubled youth.

Death, Life, and Philosophy: The Trolley Problem

Decisions involving a choice of evils can be illustrated by the classic trolley problem: a trolley or train on its rails loses its breaks and will crash into five (or four, three, or two) people on the tracks, unless the driver deliberately diverts it onto an adjoining track, which will result in the killing of just one person. Does the driver have the right to willfully chose to kill one innocent person if that is the only way to prevent the deaths of two or more people? I have been teaching that problem in varying forms for more than fifty years, well in advance of the trolley problem being constructed by philosophers as a thought experiment. It was anticipated in the Talmud 2,000 years ago, in a situation where an enemy threatens to destroy an entire city unless one innocent person is turned over to be sacrificed. This hypothetical case became tragic reality during the Holocaust.

Years before 9/11, I presented my students with the following choices of evils: an airplane has been hijacked and its radio shut down by the hijackers; it is over the ocean flying in the direction of the Empire State Building; if it is shot down now before it flies over populated areas, it is certain that 300 passengers and crew will die; if it is not shot down, there is a 90 (80, 70, 50?) percent chance that 5,000 people will die. That catastrophe is not 100 percent certain, because there is always a possibility that the passengers will regain control. Should the plane be shot down? This hypothetical, too, almost became reality during the 9/11 hijacking, when a plane flying toward the capital crashed before the decision whether to shoot it down had to be made.

There are no perfect answers to these choices of lethal evil questions. That is why they make for such good classroom discussions. In a real-world democracy, the salient question is <u>who</u> decides, since reasonable people can and do disagree as to <u>which</u> decision is right.

When Rights Clash

This is an especially difficult conundrum when rights clash. A recent example of conflicting rights involves the right to protest in front of the homes of justices and other public figures, versus the right of these individuals to be secure against harassment, intimidation, and other threats to their safety. The near assassination of Justice Kavanaugh brought that issue to a head. The White House refused to condemn or even criticize boisterous protesters who tried to interfere with Kavanaugh's dinner by shouting outside a steak house in which he was eating. The press secretary said they had "a right" to protest, without indicating whether the president believes they "were right" to exercise that "right" in the manner they did. It is not always <u>right</u> to <u>exercise</u> a right. The Nazis had a right to march in Skokie, but they were wrong to do so. The same was true of the racists in Charlottesville, who exercised the right of free speech by shouting "Jews will not replace us" and other racist slogans.

When the government decides these tragic choices, they are asked to do so by first determining whether a "right" is involved, because rights trump mere interests, just as constitutional restrictions trump legislative and executive actions. But there is often a dispute over whether a particular interest is a right—constitutional, religious, natural, or otherwise. Abortion advocates believe that pregnant women have a constitutional right to choose, at least at some points during their pregnancy. Abortion opponents believe that the fetus has a constitutional right to life. Some believe that neither has constitutional rights, only interests. But even if there are rights on both sides, they are in conflict, as rights and interests often are. And the resolution of such conflicts, in a democracy governed by the rule of law, requires us to determine who gets to decide these legal, intellectual, and moral issues: which interest qualify as rights that generally trump interests; and if there are conflicting rights, which prevails?

Victimless Rights versus Rights with Victims

For purposes of discussion, it may be useful to distinguish three categories of rights: those with direct victims; those with no victims; and those with indirect possible victims. This trichotomy can be illustrated by reference to the conflicting claims over abortion, gay marriage, and gun possession.

Following Justice Alito's majority decision overruling *Roe v. Wade*, many advocates of abortion rights expressed fear that other relatively new rights, based on privacy, might be in danger. These endangered rights include birth control, interracial marriage, and gay marriage. Though it is clear that opponents of these rights will seek to have them overruled based on the "logic" of the *Roe* overruling, it is questionable whether they will succeed. (As Justice Oliver Wendell Holmes reminded us: "The life of the law has not been logic: it has been experience.") It is true that all of these rights are based, at least in part, on the constitutionally unenumerated right of privacy, but there is a considerable difference among them—a difference that should give the justices considerable pause before sliding down a slippery slope toward diminishing the fundamental right to be "let alone," which Justice Louis Brandeis characterized as our "most important" liberty.

The critical difference is that the rights to use birth control and to marry whomever one loves <u>do not clash with any other rights</u> or even legitimate interests. No one is hurt when a couple seeks to prevent conception, when a Black woman marries a man of a different race, or when a man marries or has sex with another man. These acts are simply nobody's else's business—at least from a legal and constitutional point of view. According to the philosophy of John Stuart Mill—and other libertarians—the "only purpose for which [governmental] power can be rightfully exercised over any member of a civilized community, against his will, is to prevent <u>harm</u> to <u>others</u>." [emphasis added] Private sexual conduct does no "harm to others." Those engaging in such conduct have the right to be let alone because it does not conflict with any other right or legitimate interest, even for those who might be morally or religiously opposed to such alleged "sins" committed by those who don't believe they are sins.

This important point can be illustrated by a vignette from one of my speaking engagements. I was addressing a predominately Orthodox Jewish audience and advocating equal rights for gay people, including the right to have sex and to marry. An obviously Orthodox woman was recognized during the question period and made the following point: "I have the right to oppose gay sex and marriage, because whenever I think about two men having sex together, I get disgusted. And the government should protect me against being disgusted by sinful acts." I then asked her the following impolite question: "When you have sex with your husband, are you on top or on bottom?" The audience gasped at the chutzpah of my question, and she responded defiantly, "How dare you! That is none of your business." To which I responded, "Aha." She asked what I meant by "Aha." I replied: "If it is none of <u>my</u> business how <u>you</u> have sex in private, then why is it <u>your</u> business if two men have sex in private?" The audience gave me a standing ovation. And she walked out.

This vignette illustrates the Supreme Court's pre-<u>Roe</u> decision declaring birth control to be a constitutionally protected right. Many of those who opposed the birth control clinic in New Haven during the early 1960s also claimed to be offended by the fact that they knew that inside the door of that clinic, and in the bedrooms of the married couples who were patients, a sinful act—namely, the use of birth control—was being practiced. The fact that it was being practiced by people who didn't accept the religious prohibition of the protestors led the High Court to recognize the right of privacy over the objections of those who were offended by the private use of birth control.

Another example of a victimless right that some courts and legislators have refused to recognize is the right to die with dignity. It is no one's business but that of the person involved and his family and friends. If a sane, rational, and thoughtful adult decides to end his or her life, he or she should be entitled to do so without governmental interference. Consider for example the decision made by Mark Fleishman, the former owner of Studio 54 in New York, in July 2022. He had been suffering for several years from a degenerative illness that made his life unbearable. He thought hard about it, consulted with many people, and decided to end his life at age eighty-two. He did not want to ask anybody to help him, because assisting suicide is deemed criminal in many states, and he did not want to get anyone else in trouble.

In Chapter 6, I describe one of my own cases in which the husband of a terminally ill woman who helped her commit suicide was prosecuted for murder. We won, but not before an expensive and emotionally draining trial. In order to avoid such a legal entanglement, Mr. Fleishman decided to go to a clinic in Switzerland that helps people die with dignity. It was his decision, and no one should have been permitted to stop him from acting on it. But in 1997 the Supreme Court upheld the power of states to criminalize assisted suicide, reasoning that governments have an interest in protecting life and avoiding the slippery slope from suicide to euthanasia. They rejected the notion that a terminally ill person has a "liberty" interest in determining his own time and manner of death. They were wrong. There is no liberty more fundamental than the right to make one's own death and life decisions when no one else has a conflicting right.

Abortion is different, at least for those who regard the fetus as actual human life. For them, fetuses are "others" who are deserving of protection by the state. For those who do not regard the fetus as human life, abortion is another victimless right. Indeed, the very decision to include abortion in a book about "death" and "killing" is controversial, because many pro-choice advocates do not regard the termination of pregnancies as deaths or killing. I decided to include abortion because without the right to abort, some pregnant women will die. Moreover, I cannot simply ignore the belief by many that abortion, certainly in the late term, does include "death" and "killing."

Even those who do not hold such views, the decision to abort a fetus, particularly one that is several months old, is not like the decision to remove an appendix or tonsils. A fetus is a something, not a nothing, even for those of us who believe that a woman has the right not always to carry it to term and birth it. An infected appendix is a nothing, not worthy of a moment's reflection. No one ever regretted or had moral qualms about removing an appendix. Yet some advocates of abortion equate a fetus to an infected appendix. Florence Kennedy, a pioneer in litigating abortion cases (and a friend), made the following statement in the runup to *Roe v. Wade*. "There is no need for any legislation on abortion just as there is no need for legislation on an appendectomy."

This analogy, and others like it, are common among abortion advocates, but it does not reflect the view of most Americans. Nor does it reflect the views of most justices who have voted in favor of a woman's right to choose to abort a fetus at some point in pregnancy. It is a mistake—tactically, legally, and morally—to ignore the difference between a fetus (especially a viable one) and an appendix. The case for abortion must take into account the widespread belief that ending the existence of a fetus, especially after a few months, involves a clash of rights and interests—a clash that should be resolved in favor of the pregnant woman, but one that is not without countervailing rights and interests. Failure to recognize the difference between mid- and late-term abortion on the one hand and the removal of an appendix on the other hand will increase the likelihood that those who want to overrule privacy rights without victims will gain strength from the false comparison. The right to marry whom one loves and to use birth control is legally and morally closer to the right to remove an appendix, in that neither is anyone's business other than the individuals involved. Abortion is different and should be so regarded.

As with most complicated moral, medical, and legal issues, the question of when life begins is very much a matter of degree and opinion. Immediately upon conception, a zygote is created. It is a eukaryotic cell formed by the fertilization between two gametes. It lasts for several days until it become a blastocyst, which then develops into an embryo. Only an extremist would regard these collections of cells formed just days earlier as a "human being" or "person," subject to the same legal or moral protections as a child who has been born. It is a "something"—the earliest stages of a <u>potential</u> human life—but it is very different, both in kind and degree from a person who has been born. The legal and moral question is whether this early collection of cells, which does not resemble a human being or share its characteristics of consciousness or feelings, is more like a person or an appendix for purposes of rendering a decision whether its progress toward <u>becoming</u> a human being can be terminated by the person in whose body it is. That person could have decided (in most cases) not to create the zygote or blastocyst; does she now have the right to decide to end its development into a fetus at this early stage, or does the government have the power to compel her to bear an unwanted child?

These questions become more difficult as the pregnancy proceeds through its several stages. For some on both sides, there are no matters of degree: extremists on the "pro-life" side regard the day-old zygote as a human being; extremists on the choice side regard a viable eight-month fetus as an appendix. There are many more of the former than the latter. The vast majority of those who advocate choice do not support very late-term abortion of viable fetuses if there is an alternative.

It is difficult to regard abortion at the earliest stages—which is primarily performed medically, by pills, rather than surgically—as "killing" a "victim" but is so regarded by pro-life extremists. And it is difficult to regard the surgical abortion of viable eight-month fetus as no different from the removal of an appendix.

It is the extremes on both sides—those who falsely believe that a fetus is no different from a live human being, and those who falsely believe that a fetus, regardless of stage, is no different from an appendix—who seem to agree that if *Roe* is overruled, it is only logical that other privacy rights, such as contraception and marriage, will be overruled. Both are wrong. Courts should be more willing to recognize rights that in no way impinge on other rights than they are if they believe that by recognizing one alleged right (abortion) they may be undercutting another (the so-called right to life). Accordingly, the case for overruling conception and marriage rights is far weaker than the weak (at least in my view) case for having overruled the half-century-old-precedent of *Roe*.

My prediction, therefore, is that the Supreme Court will not necessarily compound the mistake of overruling *Roe* by overruling privacy rights that pose no conflict with other rights or legitimate interests. Only the false "logic" of the extremes on both sides—those who believe that a fetus is a person and those who believe it is an appendix—compels the same result in these very different cases.

The courts will probably not base their decisions overtly on my proposed distinction between "victimless rights"—a term I have coined—and rights with possible victims, but this commonsense distinction, based on both logic and experience, will probably influence their thinking. It certainly should.

Now compare these rights—abortion, which has a potential "victim," versus marriage rights, which has no victim—with the right to own a gun. The Second Amendment, as interpreted by the current Supreme Court, grants individuals the right "to keep and bear arms." This right, unlike abortion, has no <u>direct</u> and <u>immediate</u> victims: there is no one-to-one relationship between the right to own a gun and someone being shot, as there is between an abortion and the death of a fetus. The vast majority of guns are not used to commit homicide. But a significant number of homicides are committed with the assistance of guns legally obtained under the Second Amendment, such as the one used to kill seven people and injure many more in Highland Park. So unlike marriage rights, which have no conceivable victims, direct or indirect, or abortion which has direct "victims," if one regards the fetus as subject to victimhood, gun rights have at least the possibility of causing death or injury to some victims even if they may also save some lives. Gun rights, therefore, fall into an intermediate category on the continuum of rights with or without victims.

Criminal defendants' rights, especially those like the exclusionary rule that may sometimes free guilty murderers, may also have indirect victims. So may the abolition of the death penalty, which is imposed on guilty murderers—at least in theory—to protect innocent lives by deterring murder. So, this, too, is an intermediate case under the victimless paradigm.

Capital punishment is also intended to impose morally appropriate punishment—"life for life"—on the guilty murderer under the principle of "lex talionis." Opponents of capital punishment argue that it is immoral for the state deliberately to take a human life. I now believe—having earlier in my life believed the opposite—that the strictly moral case against capital punishment is problematic. There are, of course, strong moral arguments against the state taking human life. But despite the arguments that have been made throughout history, every state has taken, or authorized the taking of, lives: in war, in self-defense, and by engaging in or permitting useful construction or other activities, such as driving or smoking, that carry the inevitable risk of death. In general, moral states have balanced the cost of taking some human lives against the benefits of saving others. This is the context in which capital punishment should be morally evaluated.

Is Capital Punishment Immoral?

I have opposed capital punishment since I could think and speak. I opposed the execution of the Rosenbergs, who were accused of spying for the Soviet Union. As a young teenager I signed a petition seeking to save their lives. I even opposed the execution of Adolph Eichmann, who was responsible for the death of hundreds of thousands of Jews. My first published letter to the editor argued in favor of life imprisonment for this mass murderer. As a high school and college debate champion, I argued forcibly against the death penalty. In our home, we have posters protesting the death penalty imposed on Sacco and Vanzetti, the Scottsboro defendants, and the Rosenbergs. But as a teacher of criminal law, I always played the devil's advocate, espousing positions contrary to those taken by the majority of students. I did not express my own view on the death penalty, but rather forced my students to defend their views against my unforgiving criticisms. Sometimes this exercise persuaded me to change my mind.

Let me illustrate my devil's advocate approach by replicating the class I would often teach regarding capital punishment and the law.

I would begin by asking my 150 students: "How many of you are opposed to capital punishment on strictly moral grounds?" A substantial majority of students would raise their hands. I would then press a little further: "Are you absolutely certain that your opposition to capital punishment is purely moral, and not empirical?" A few hands would go down, but the majority would still remain up.

I would then turn to one of the students who seemed most enthusiastic in his moral opposition to the death penalty and challenge him: "I don't think your opposition is based on moral grounds!" He would respond angrily: "Yes, it is," sometimes adding, "How dare you question my morality." I would then say, "Let me prove to you that your opposition is not entirely moral. Indeed, it isn't moral at all." The student would cross his arms defiantly as if to say, "Okay, prove to me that my long moral opposition to the death penalty isn't true."

I would then begin my Socratic exercise. "What if I could prove to you, conclusively and beyond any doubt, that by executing one obviously guilty murderer, society could save the lives of ten innocent future murder victims?" The student would respond: "There is no way you can prove that, and it isn't true." I would reply that moral discourse requires consideration of hypothetical situations without regard to the actual evidence: that in order to test your claim that your objection is purely moral, I am entitled to present you with a hypothetical set of facts, and you are not entitled to dispute my hypothetical scenario. I would remind him of the trolley example, which requires students to address an extremely unlikely hypothetical scenario. The student is not entitled to say: "I would try to drive the train off the track so that I would be killed instead of the five or the one." That option is not in the hypothetical. There is no third choice. I would then insist that the student answer the question: Would it be moral to execute one clearly guilty criminal if by doing so, and only by doing so, the state could prevent the death of ten innocent potential murder victims? If the answer is yes, or even maybe, then the case for a strict moral opposition is weakened: The opposition depends, at least to some degree, on whether the factual assumptions underlying my hypothetical are empirically provable.

I would then open the conversation beyond that one student to the entire class, beginning by asking how many of them think it would be morally correct for the train engineer to divert his unstoppable trolley or train onto the track with one innocent dying in order to save five innocents? The vast majority of students would agree that that was the moral thing to do. A few Kantians and moral absolutists would allow the five to die, in order to save the engineer from the moral hazard of the utilitarian decision to kill an innocent person.

I would then ask the students who voted to save the five how that is different from my death penalty hypothetical. Indeed, I would insist that my hypothetical is easier, because the executed man to be killed is guilty of murder! He took at least one human life. (One could amplify the hypothetical by requiring that the capital defendant be guilty of two or more murders, like Nikolas Cruz, who pleaded guilty to murdering seventeen students and faculty at a Parkland school.) So, if it is moral to take the life of one innocent track-sitter to avoid the death of five innocent track-sitters, why isn't it entirely moral to take the life of a single mass murderer in order to save not five, but ten innocent people? Again, I would ask for a show of hands. This time fewer than half would agree that executing the murderer would be immoral if he were clearly guilty and his execution would save ten innocent lives.

I would then ask for a volunteer from among those who believed that the engineer should kill the innocent person to save five, but that the state should not kill the guilty murderer to save ten. The volunteer would generally say that there is a difference between the state killing someone, even a guilty defendant in a calculated manner, and an individual making an inevitably tragic choice decision in the moment. I would respond: "But I am asking you whether the state should pass a carefully calculated law or establish a precedent explicitly authorizing an engineer to choose the life of one over the lives of five. So, the state is acting in calculated fashion in both instances.

Other students would say that the death penalty is different from the trolley case, because the trolley situation is extremely unlikely to occur, whereas murders and the death penalty are recurring. I would respond that although the precise trolley example is unlikely, there are numerous other examples of the state authorizing the death of the few to save the lives of many. In addition to war, these include widespread mandatory inoculations against smallpox and other deadly diseases, which inevitably result in a small number of deaths of those vaccinated and a large number of smallpox deaths prevented.

I would then ask the students if they would accept as a general principle that it is morally permissible for the state to take one life in order to prevent one-plus number of deaths, provided that the evidence was near-certain. Most students would agree with that proposition, though a few would still disagree. Some would say, "Since I could never be the one to administer the lethal injection to the guilty murderer, I cannot demand that others do it. My response is that the claim that a particular person cannot kill another person is a psychological, not a moral one. There are many things that are morally permissible that some of us could not do, such as inserting the cylinder of a ballpoint pen into the trachea of a choking person in order to save his life. That is the morally correct thing to do, though it may be psychologically impossible for some moral people to do it. It would seem to follow that if it is morally permissible to execute the guilty murderer, it wouldn't matter that many individuals would be psychologically incapable of doing it.

A clever student would inevitably come up with the following ploy: "Why not simply announce that you have executed the guilty criminal, so that it will have its intended deterrent effect, but actually keep him hidden until he dies a natural death?" I would respond by saying that this raises an entirely different but related issue, namely: When is it proper to lie in order to save lives, especially if the liar is the state? I would tell a true story related to me by my friend the late Professor Monroe Friedman, whose Rabbi had been summoned for jury duty in a capital murder case. The question the Rabbi put to the professor is: "I have a strong moral opposition to the death penalty based on my religious beliefs. I also have a strong opposition to lying based on my religious beliefs. I have been asked in my jury questionnaire whether I am morally opposed to the death penalty. If I truthfully answer yes, I will be disqualified for service on the capital case. If I falsely answer no, I may be picked to serve on that jury and I will surely vote against the death penalty, thus saving a life." The Rabbi then asked the professor: "Should I lie to possibly save a human life?" Professor Friedman took the easy way out saying, "As a lawyer I can't advise to you to commit perjury," implying that this was a moral choice the Rabbi had to make for himself. The Rabbi was not picked for the jury, but his hypothetical question remains relevant to our discussion.

In the Cruz case, some of the nine jurors who voted for the death penalty have implicitly accused some of the three who voted against it—unanimity is required—of being untruthful in saying they had an open mind before deliberating.

In the end, most of us who are strongly opposed to capital punishment have come to that conclusion based on a combination of moral, empirical, psychological, religious, and other values that are hard to separate from one another. I think it may be true that under certain circumstances imposing the death penalty on one guilty criminal may actually save some lives. I believe that the death penalty, under some circumstances, can actually deter conduct. One extreme example will suffice to show that it is at least possible.

Near the end of the Second World War, Nazi troops continued to occupy cities in Denmark. The Nazi occupiers passed a law that everyone must use blackout shades to prevent allied bombers from identifying city targets. Anyone who violated this law would be punished by long imprisonment. But many continued to light up their windows, knowing that no amount of imprisonment would actually exceed a few weeks, because Denmark would soon be liberated, and all Nazi prisoners freed. But as soon as the Nazi occupiers announced that violation of the blackout laws would result in the immediate imposition of the death penalty, all the shades were pulled down. The point is that the death penalty sometimes deters more effectively than short imprisonment. This historical vignette does not prove that the death penalty deters more effectively than life imprisonment, but it contradicts the argument that the death penalty <u>never</u> deters.

Even those who agree that the death penalty deters quarrel with the assumption that under current laws and practices all defendants subject to the death penalty are in fact guilty, and that all lives saved are in fact innocent. The requirement of proof beyond a reasonable doubt leaves open the possibility that some innocent defendants may be convicted. And some of the lives saved may be those of gang members, mafiosi, and other not-so-innocent people.

Moreover, the death penalty has never been administered fairly. Good lawyers almost never lose their clients to the executioner. In more than a half century of practice, I haven't,[2] and neither have any of my highly qualified lawyer friends and associates. In most parts of the United States, the death penalty is reserved for indigent defendants who lack the resources to retain excellent lawyers, investigators, and other necessary members of a success-ful defense team. There are also racial and gender considerations at play. The death penalty is more likely to be imposed on Black defendants who are convicted of murdering white victims than on white defendants convicted of murdering Black victims. The same is true of women; men are more likely to be executed for murder-ing women than women are for murdering men. Other invidious factors may also distort the process of imposing the death penalty fairly.

In 1972, the Supreme Court in *Furman v. Georgia* struck down then-existing death penalty laws, declaring them cruel and unusual

---

2   I was unable to persuade President Trump to commute the death sentence of a Black man who, as a teenager, had participated in the murder of a young couple. He was not my client, and I made one phone call on his behalf, just before his scheduled execution. Trump's refusal was still devastating to me. The contrast between his execution and the life sentence imposed on Nikolas Cruz will illustrate the lack of consistency in who gets the death penalty.

punishment. I played a role in that decision, as described in Chapter 5. Several states then revised their laws to reduce the kind of discretion that made the imposition of the death penalty as random as "being struck by lightning," to quote the imprecise metaphor cited by Justice Potter Stewart. Subsequently, the High Court upheld some of these statutes, and defendants began again to be executed, though in smaller numbers than previously.

When all of these considerations are factored in, the case against the death penalty becomes strengthened beyond a purely moral or logical case. Experience with the death penalty is an important factor.

Despite the limitations of morality and logic, my Socratic exercise can do some good. Actual experience with how unfairly the death penalty works in practice is more convincing than the logic of my Socratic methods. Under the current rules governing jury selection, no one can serve who has a moral opposition to the death penalty. Pursuant to the analysis presented in my Socratic class, if one of my students is now called to jury duty and asked if she has a purely moral opposition to the death penalty, she can honestly answer no, even if she is strongly opposed to capital punishment based on multiple factors not limited to morality.

The above analysis, made in the context of the death penalty, can also be applied to other life/death choices, such as wars, the targeting of terrorists, the use of deadly force by the police, and even abortion.

Logic and Experience

Consider for example abortion, which many advocates on both sides believe is a purely moral issue. Some (but not all) opponents of abortion admit that if there is a choice of saving the life of the mother or the life of the fetus, it is morally permissible to save the life of the mother. Under Jewish law, that choice is mandatory, since Jewish law explicitly prefers saving a living human over saving a potential human being, though it values both "lives." Many (but not all) proponents of a woman's choice to have an abortion would limit that choice based on the state of the pregnancy. They would argue that a woman should not be allowed to choose to abort an eight-month fetus that would be viable outside of her womb. Either she should be forced to bear the child to term or be required to allow surgery to remove it alive from her womb.

For most (but not all) reasonable people, even the abortion decision is subject to a cost-benefit analysis, based in part on empirical factors that may change with medical and technological developments. Again, experience is more compelling than logic: the experience many pregnant women have had when abortion has been criminalized—back-alley botched procedures and other negative consequences—have persuaded some who have moral concerns about abortion to oppose criminalization. For others, the fact that most abortions today are medical, rather than surgical, and are accomplished by pills early in the pregnancy has changed minds. But for many, any decision to end a pregnancy at any state and by any means is equivalent to murder. These views are unlikely to be changed by experience—or by judicial pronouncements.

As with many tragic choices in a democracy, governed by the rule of law, the most compelling question is not <u>which</u> choice should be made, but rather <u>who</u> should be empowered to make it.

As to abortion, should it be the women aided by her doctors? Should the husband or potential father have a say in that choice? Should the government have any role? If so, which governmental institution should participate in the decision making: federal or state, legislative or judicial?

Tragic choices by their nature rarely have one correct answer. Wrong choices will inevitably be made, regardless of who makes them. In a democracy governed by the rule of law, the real question is who has the legitimate power to make these tragic choices—and the inevitable mistakes.

Warfare and the Law

Another example is the decision to engage in warfare, such as by Russia against Ukraine. That decision was made by tyrannical leaders, with no democratic input. Under our Constitution, only Congress may declare war, but the realities of modern warfare have resulted in this direct and unambiguous limitation of power being circumvented by presidents who—since the end of World War II—have ordered the waging of war and other military actions against North Korea, North Vietnam, Iraq, Afghanistan, Panama, Grenada, and others without Congress actually declaring war. They have employed euphemisms to redefine "war" and "declare" so as to transfer from the legislature to the executive the power to send fighting armies, Navies, Air Force, and cyberwarriors into battle.

There may be times when a president, as commander in chief, must order military action quickly, without time to secure congressional approval, but that was not the case in recent, well-planned military adventures. Even when the president must act quickly, the Constitution would seem to require post facto approval by Congress, such as that which occurred in the aftermath of the bombing of Pearl Harbor and the immediate military response ordered by President Roosevelt but quickly followed by a congressional declaration of war. No full-scale, long-term military action should ever be undertaken without express approval by Congress. Otherwise, the constitutional grant of authority to Congress "to declare war" would become a dead letter in violation of the intent of the Framers.

Deadly Force by Police

Another area of death-or-life decision making involved the use of deadly force by police officers. The decision to shoot may cost life, but so may the decision not to shoot. Here, too, a key question is <u>who</u> decides. At one level, the immediate choice must inevitably be made in real time by the armed officer whose life may hang in the balance. But government makes the rules for when lethal force may and may not be used. For example, in the 1985 case of *Tennessee v. Gardner*, the Supreme Court ruled that the Fourth Amendment prohibits police officers from employing deadly force in certain circumstances that include arresting a fleeing felon who poses no danger of serious physical harm. The majority opinion stated that "It is not better that all felony suspects die than that they escape"

This formulation fails to answer the really difficult questions posed by real-life encounters: when in the course of a police-suspect confrontation, is deadly force permitted or prohibited? How certain must the police officer be that the suspect poses a danger to him or her? What if the danger is to others? How imminent must it be? What if the escaping suspect in a shooting has his gun in his pocket and may possibly use it again if he is not stopped? What if the suspect is unarmed but has a history of rape or molestation? What if the officer makes an honest and reasonable mistake, such as Officer Kim Potter, who intended to tase the fleeing suspect but pulled out the wrong weapon and mistakenly shot him? What if the officer didn't shoot the subject but subdued him by employing a lethal choke hold, as in the George Floyd case?

These and other situations call for both rules and the exercise of discretion. There are no perfect answers, especially in the context of racial tensions that make objective analyses more challenging. Here, too, it must be determined who gets to make the ultimate death-life decisions: local civilian review boards, state legislatures, federal officials, or courts?

Death and Race

There are several important relationships between race and death: early death, from multiple causes, is more frequent among some racial groups than others; victimization by murder and criminal assaults disproportionately affect certain racial groups; since most violent crimes (random mass shootings being an exception) are committed by people in close proximity to their victims, it follows that a disproportionate number of murders and assaults are committed by persons who share characteristics, including race, with victims; certain racial groups are subject disproportionately to improper arrests and shootings by law enforcement officers. These are empirical conclusions, subject to changing circumstances, and they do not establish direct causal relationships with race itself: there are too many variables, such as poverty, lack of educational opportunity, familial issues, neighborhoods neglected by government, easy availability of guns, drugs, police, judicial bias, and others.

In seeking to reduce racial disparities in crime-related phenomena, all of these factors must be taken into account. It is a proper and important function of government to protect its citizens from violent predation, especially death, and also to protect its citizens from unfair governmental responses, also especially death. These issues must be high on any agenda dealing with death-life issues.

The Invasion of Ukraine

The war in Ukraine presents issues of a different dimension. There is no legal, moral, or other justification for Russia's unprovoked invasion of an independent nation and its deliberate targeting of civilians. One question is whether the massive targeting and killing of civilians amounts to genocide (see Chapter 3). A related question is whether the law can do anything to deter such outrageous behavior or help to bring it to a stop.

The International Criminal Court (ICC) was created for this purpose, but its jurisdiction and power are limited, especially with regard to nations that are not signatories, such as Russia and Belarus. (The United States, Israel, and Ukraine are not signatories either, though Ukraine has submitted to its jurisdiction.) The ICC has no jurisdiction over countries, but only over individuals. That court and others that were set up to deal with regional wars have prosecuted and convicted individual political and military leaders, as well as soldiers. These trials generally took place well after hostilities ended, as did the Nuremberg Trials following World War II. Even though neither Russia nor Ukraine is a member of the ICC, prosecutors claim jurisdiction over individual Russian war criminals and are likely to seek to prosecute them, if they can. It is unlikely, however, that any actions by the Court will prevent or deter future unlawful aggressions by Russia or other comparable law violators. The law has rarely if ever influenced the conduct of nations regarding war and peace. Even the Nuremberg trials of Nazi war criminals did not seem to deter subsequent genocides in Cambodia, Darfur, and other parts of the world.

Vaccine Mandates

A current public health example of death-and-life decisions is whether the government can mandate vaccines or other medical interventions to prevent the spread of potentially lethal diseases such as smallpox, polio, and COVID. Every medical treatment entails some risk of death. So does <u>not</u> having the treatment—not only to the person not inoculated, but to others, as well. The government must strike a balance, as must every individual who has a choice regarding treatment.

I have written a book—*The Case for Vaccine Mandates*—dealing with these complex issues, and I will not rehash my arguments here. Since writing that book, I have acquired a letter from General George Washington to his officers written in 1777 instructing them to inoculate all their troops against smallpox and telling them this is of utmost importance. Thus, the recognition that some inoculations may be required for some people—despite the risks to them—has been part of our history since the founding. This does not automatically translate into a precedent for today's more complex decisions, but it is part of our collective experience.

Political Assassinations

Recently, politically assassination has been in the news with the murder of former Japanese Prime Minister Shinzo Abe. Past political assassinations in the United States include Lincoln, Garfield, John and Robert Kennedy, and Martin Luther King Jr. Other assassinations included Archduke Franz Ferdinand, Leon Trotsky, Salvador Allende, Yitzhak Rabin, Anwar Sadat, and Alexander Litvinenko.

Some of these assassinations—Lincoln, Ferdinand, Allende, and Rabin in particular—may have changed the course of history. Some not so much. As to yet others, it may be "too early to say"—a variation on the famous, but apparently mistranslated, quote attributed to Zhou Enlai about the impact of the French Revolution.

There have also been military and quasi-military assassinations, such as the targeted killings of nuclear scientists and terrorist leaders by Israel, as well as the killing of Osama bin Ladin and other terrorists by the United States.

As I have shown in my prior books on the subject, the law of war is ambiguous and unclear when it comes to targeted killings of enemies. Actual combatants who are engaged in ongoing belligerent acts are fair game for assassination. So are those who command others to do so. A harder issue concerns scientists and technicians who help develop weapons to be used unlawfully against civilian targets. Another hard issue involved part-time terrorists and combatants who are civilians by day and terrorists by night. Can they be targeted when they are not engaging in terrorist activities?

As with other issues of death and life, a balance must be struck between preventing the deaths of innocent civilians and avoiding the killing of questionable combatants.

An issue related to terrorism that also requires the striking of such a balance involves the use of pressure tactics, including torture, to produce real-time intelligence calculated to prevent deadly terrorist attacks. Both torture and terrorism can cause death and serious injury, and in some instances the use of torture can prevent terrorism. Accordingly, scholars and commentators have debated whether it is ever justified to use torture to prevent terrorism. Jeremy Bentham presented the following utilitarian argument justifying torture in certain situations:

> Suppose an occasion were to arise, in which a suspicion is entertained, as strong as that which would be received as a sufficient ground for arrest and commitment as for felony—a suspicion that at this very time a considerable number of individuals are actually suffering, by illegal violence inflictions equal in intensity to those which if inflicted by the hand of justice, would universally be spoken of under the name of torture. For the purpose of rescuing from torture these hundred innocents, should any scruple be made of applying equal or superior torture, to extract the requisite information from the mouth of one criminal, who having it in his power to make known the place where at this time the enormity was practicing or about to be practiced, should refuse to do so? To say nothing of wisdom, could any pretense be made so much as to the praise of blind and vulgar humanity, by the man who to save one criminal, should determine to abandon 100 innocent persons to the same fate?

Other philosophers strongly disagree. Contemporary jurist Ben Juratowich argues:

That is a crucial point: the successful torturer causes his victims to suffer and then uses her suffering against herself for socially beneficial ends. The tortured person is reduced to a suffering instrument of the torturer. Her life may be preserved and in fact it is necessary for her life to be preserved so that it can be put to use in the way desired by others—but her dignity and autonomy are completely disrespected. It is for this reason that torture is properly labeled barbaric and for this reason that torture is something that the state should not inflict on any human, by virtue of her humanity. Because torturing someone is, when viewed as an act in and of itself, so abhorrent, it does not qualify as something that may be put on the scales to balance against other things that we would like to avoid.[3]

By this same "logic," the trolley driver must let the five be killed, because to kill the one to save the five would be to use her as an "instrument." This Kantian argument ignores the reality that people are constantly and properly used as "instruments" to effect a net saving of lives.

I have written extensively and controversially about this cost-benefit issue. My personal view is that "I oppose torture as a normative matter," as I have repeatedly said and written. But as an empirical matter, I know that governments—including our own, Israel, and other Western democracies—sometimes employ it. So, I proposed that a useful way to limit and perhaps end its use is to require a "torture warrant" to be issued by a judge based on extreme necessity. Here is what I have written:

All forms of torture are widespread among nations that have signed treaties prohibiting all torture. The current situation is unacceptable: it tolerates torture without accountability and encourages hypocritical posturing. I would like to see improvement in the current situation by reducing or eliminating torture,

3 Juratowitch, Ben, 2008, "Torture Is Always Wrong," *Public Affairs Quarterly*, Vol. 22, No. 2, p. 87.

while increasing viability and accountability. I am opposed to torture as a normative matter, but I know it is taking place today
and believe that it would certainly be employed if we ever expe-
rienced an imminent threat of mass casualty biological, chemical,
or nuclear terrorism.

[I]f torture is being or will be practiced, is it worse to close our
eyes to it and tolerate its use by low-level law enforcement officials without accountability, or instead to bring it to the surface by
requiring that a warrant of some kind be required as a precondition
to the infliction of any type of torture under any circumstances?

This proposal has been widely misunderstood as a justification for torture. It is not. It is a severe restriction on its use. It is also an attempt
to answer the question I <u>always</u> ask about controversial issues: In a
democracy, <u>who</u> decides the matter of conflicting rights and interest?
Here is what I have written about that important decision:

As I pointed out in *Why Terrorism Works*, several important values
are pitted against each other in this conflict. The first is the safety
and security of a nation's citizens. Under the ticking bomb scenario this value may be thought to require the use of torture, if that
were the only way to prevent the ticking bomb from exploding and
killing large numbers of civilians. The second value is the preservation of civil liberties and human rights. This value requires that
we not accept torture as a legitimate part of our legal system. In
my debates with two prominent civil libertarians, Floyd Abrams
and Harvey Silverglate, both acknowledged that they would want
non-lethal torture to be used if it could prevent thousands of deaths,
but they did not want torture to be officially recognized by our
legal system. As Floyd Abrams put it: "In a democracy sometimes it
is necessary to do things off the books and below the radar screen."
Former presidential candidate Alan Keyes took the position that
although torture might be necessary in a given situation, it could
never be right. He suggested that a president should authorize the
torturing of a ticking bomb terrorist, but that this act should not
be legitimated by the courts or incorporated into our legal system.

He argued that wrongful and indeed unlawful acts might sometimes be necessary to preserve the nation, but that no aura of legitimacy should be placed on these actions by judicial imprimatur. This understandable approach is in conflict with a third important value: namely, open accountability and visibility in a democracy. "Off-the-book actions below the radar screen" are antithetical to the theory and practice of democracy. Citizens cannot approve or disapprove of governmental actions of which they are unaware. We have learned the lesson of history that off-the-book actions can produce terrible consequences. Former President Richard Nixon's creation of a group of "plumbers" led to Watergate, and former President Ronald Reagan's authorization of an "off-the-books" foreign policy in Central American led to the Iran-Contra scandal. And these are only the ones we know about!

In a democracy governed by a rule of law, we should never want our soldiers or president to take any action, which we deem wrong or illegal. A good test of whether an action should or should not be done is whether we are prepared to have it disclosed, perhaps not immediately, but certainly after some time has passed. No legal system operating under the rule of law should ever tolerate an "off-the-books" approach to necessity. Even the defense of necessity must be justified lawfully. The road to tyranny has always been paved with claims of necessity made by those responsible for the security of a nation. Our system of checks and balances requires that all presidential actions, like all legislative or military actions, be consistent with governing law. If it is necessary to torture in the ticking bomb case, then our governing laws must accommodate this practice. If we refuse to change our law to accommodate any particular action, then our government should not take that action. Requiring that a controversial action be made openly and with accountability is one way of minimizing resort to unjustifiable means.

The decision to use or not use extreme interrogation measures including torture is often a matter of death and life—for the innocent victims of the tortured terrorist or for the often-guilty victim of torture. Who gets to make that tragic-choice decision—on both the macro and micro level—is critical to the rule of law.

The Role of Law in Reducing Deaths

In sum, the law of death and life is among the most important aspects of our legal system. In some areas, the law has a powerful impact on causing or preventing death. In other areas, less so. Sometimes the impact is direct. Sometimes indirect. But in every situation, the law plays some role in deciding who shall die and who shall live. In general, the law follows the Biblical command: "choose life." The question then becomes: whose life—and whose death? The mother or the fetus? The citizens of our nation or theirs? The innocent or the guilty? The policeman or the suspect? The many or the few? The powerful or the powerless?

Death-and-life decisions need not always be a zero-sum game, with some dying so that others might live. Sometimes the law can help prevent the deaths of people on all sides: by promoting life-saving medical research; by encouraging, or even mandating, the use of life-saving organs from cadavers; by making life-saving vaccines widely available, and mandating their use when necessary; by ending particular military conflicts; by reducing the needs for abortion; by providing better training of police officers; by providing better environmental protection; by encouraging emigration from dangerous areas; by taking measures to reduce crime and its causes; and by other win-win steps that do not pit death against life, but that favor all life over most other values.

In the chapters to come, I will elaborate on death-and-life legal decisions in several contexts.

CHAPTER I

The Supreme Court on Abortion and Gun Control

In the 2021–2022 term, the justices rendered several important death-and-life decisions regarding abortion and guns. I wrote the following op-eds about this issue in real time. I have updated them for this book.

States can't regulate guns, but they can ban abortions. Why?
The United State Supreme Court has limited substantially the power of the states to regulate the carrying of guns in public. The justices refused to recognize that different states, and different areas within states, have different needs with regard to gun control. They have ruled that one size fits all under the Second Amendment. This ignores the reality that the militia referred to within the Second Amendment were "well regulated" by the states. The words of the Constitution would certainly seem to authorize state-by-state and city-by-city differential regulation. But not for the Supreme Court, which has essentially denied states the inherent power to protect their citizens against gun violence.

The Supreme Court subsequently decided another case involving the regulation of abortions. Singing a completely different tune, the same majority that took the power to regulate guns from the states gave the power to regulate abortions back to the states. Why the difference?

Defenders of these decisions will argue that the right to bear arms is explicitly guaranteed by the Second Amendment, whereas there is no explicit reference to abortion in the Constitution. This argument goes too far. The Second Amendment itself has limiting language in the words "well-regulated militia," strongly suggesting that the states have the power to regulate gun ownership. Moreover, even though the word abortion is not in the Constitution, the Fourth Amendment guarantees the right of the people, including women, to be secure in their persons. At the time of the Framing, the word "secure" described what we today call the right of privacy.

It would seem to follow, even for a constitutional textualist, that both rights—to possess a gun in public and to end a pregnancy in private—have some basis in the Constitution. And both would seem to allow for some degree of state regulation. Absolutes are anathema to good governance. No right is ever absolute, even the freedom of speech. Nor should any right be subject to complete abrogation. Our system of federalism divides the power to regulate between the states and the federal government. Our system of checks and balances also allocates different powers to the three branches of government. The Supreme Court's decisions in the gun case and in the abortion case distort these balances.

The reality is that these decisions, both of which fly in the face of long precedents, are solely a function of numbers: after President Trump was able to nominate three justices—one of them improperly—the conservative majority is likely to prevail for a good many years. What is often ignored, however, is that the current conservative majority is anything but conservative. It is a judicially activist majority comprised of justices with agendas. They decide cases more broadly than necessary and render decisions depriving the other branches of government of their legitimate powers. What then is to be done to right these judicially imposed wrongs? In an ideal world, the Constitution would be amended to allow reasonable gun control and reasonable access to abortion. But ours is a Constitution that was deliberately designed to make amendments difficult. We have only had twenty-seven in the past two and a quarter centuries. It is unlikely that either of these two cases could make it through the difficult process. So executive and legislative actions will be required to test the limits of these dangerous decisions. But in the final analysis, the Supreme Court will have the ultimate authority to determine the limit on actions by the popularly elected branches. In a democracy the voices of the people cannot however be ignored. And both of these absolutist decisions will not be popular with a majority of Americans who support both reasonable gun control and reasonable access to abortion. This is the time for political action, not violence. It is the nature of democracy as well that you win some and lose some. We have lost a good deal with these two decisions, but the process is ongoing, and, as Martin Luther King Jr. reminded us, "Let us realize the arc of the moral universe is long, but it bends toward justice."

Face it—SCOTUS has long been partisan when deciding political cases.

The overruling of *Roe v. Wade* increases the likelihood that Democrats will try to pack the Supreme Court. The *Dobbs* is a decision widely viewed as an unprincipled act of partisan power as distinguished from a proper exercise in legal judgment. The Commission appointed by United States President Joe Biden to explore this among other options did not make a recommendation regarding court packing, though some members favored it. It will get more support from Democratic voters now that a woman's right to choose abortion has been severely curtailed. It will also diminish the standing of the High Court.

This fear was expressed by liberal members of the Court's minority and is almost certainly of deep concern to Chief Justice John Roberts. The High Court's standing in polls has dropped considerably since its transparently partisan decision in *Bush v. Gore* twenty-two years ago. Since that time, it has rendered controversial decisions, both increasing and undercutting fundamental rights such as gay marriage and religious freedom. It has also dramatically expanded gun rights. During this period, the pendulum has swung quite narrowly. Justices appointed by Republican presidents have occasionally voted with those appointed by Democratic presidents and vice versa.

This seems to be changing with the appointments of three justices in four years by then-President Donald Trump, who was open about trying to reshape the court along party lines. The influence of appointing individual justices was manifested most clearly by the debacle over the failed appointment of Merrick Garland by then-President Barack Obama and the successful appointment by Trump of Amy Coney Barrett in the run-up to the 2020 election. The decision on abortion rights surely reflects those events as well as Trump's two earlier appointments.

The fear that the Supreme Court has become a political institution indistinguishable from the two elected branches of government is partly accurate. The truth is more nuanced. The court is less likely to be partisan in the majority of its cases that represent important but largely noncontroversial legal issues, such as resolving conflicts among the circuits over statutory construction and the like. These cases form a substantial part of the court's docket. But several deeply controversial and high-profile cases are on every year's docket, and it is these cases that are often influenced by partisan appointments. That is not always the case, as evidenced by the unanimous decision—that included two Clinton appointees—back in 1998 compelling President Bill Clinton to submit to depositions in a civil case (a decision that I think was wrong). But just two years later, the court's 5–4 decision ending Al Gore's run for the presidency was transparently partisan.

So, the makeup of the docket determines how partisan and political the decisions are likely to be. This is significant because the justices determine their own docket: it takes four votes to grant review. Justice Louis Brandeis once observed that the most important decisions made by the justices are deciding not to take a case. The corollary is that a discretionary decision to take a case, as was made in the recent Mississippi abortion case, can be highly partisan and have profound consequences.

The divided decision, along partisan lines, overruling *Roe* turned the Court into a primary battlefield in the cultural wars dividing our nation. But some will argue that these wars began with *Roe v. Wade*, and it was inevitable that each side would seek victory through partisan appointments. There may be some truth to this, but there is also truth to the argument that it is better to develop a right, such as the right of privacy, over many years, as was done with regard to *Roe*, than to abrogate it based entirely on a change in the makeup of the court.

This is not the first time such an abrupt change occurred. When then-President Franklin D. Roosevelt threatened to pack the court so that his New Deal would be held constitutional, shifts occurred that upheld most of the New Deal. Historians have called it "the switch in time that saved nine." As several justices who voted to overrule *Roe* have observed, the court has previously overruled precedents of long duration, such as *Plessy v. Ferguson*, which authorized segregation, and the cases that refused to recognize gay rights. Most, but not all, of these decisions expanded constitutional rights. Overruling *Roe* contracts a woman's right to choose. Critics of *Roe* point out that it expands the fetus's right to life. That is why this decision, unlike the gay rights and gay marriage decisions, involves a class of rights, at least for those who believe that life begins at conception or shortly thereafter. Gay rights and gay marriage, on the other hand, involve no such clash. No one has a legitimate right to prevent people from making sexual and marital choices that do not involve other people.

But the argument that a fetus is a person who is entitled to the right to life goes too far—even for the justices such as Brett Kavanaugh, who would have the Supreme Court be "neutral" on abortion and leave it to the states. Under that argument, no state would have the right to deny life to a fetus, and abortions would be unconstitutional throughout America, regardless of state legislation.

But the public would never accept a national ban on all abortions. That is why pro-lifers want it left to the states, where they would get half a loaf.

Overruling or severely limiting *Roe* is among the worst instances of partisan power politics by the justices. To be sure, the five Republicans who voted to end the recount in 2000 were engaging in pure partisan politics. But at least they had the justification—perhaps excuse is a better word—that there was an emergency. As the late Justice Antonin Scalia wrote me at the time:

> Even if you think that [I] was wrong, considering the severe time
> constraint [and] the pressure to come out with a near unanimous
> opinion . . . you should cut me some slack. . . . We will talk about
> it sometime, as you say, before senility.

The Mississippi case poses no comparable emergency. Review need
not have been granted, and there was no need to go beyond deciding
whether Mississippi's ban on post-fifteen-week abortions is constitutional. *Roe* has been on the books for half a century. It should remain
the law of the land. But even after *Dobbs*, the number of justices
should remain at nine to preserve the stability of the Supreme Court
and to protect it from further politicization.

Is *Dobbs* the first case to take rights away from Americans?

Whatever one may think of *Dobbs v. Mississippi*, the Supreme Court
decision overruling *Roe v. Wade*, some critics have overstated its
uniqueness in taking from Americans their preexisting rights.
Professor Laurence Tribe badly misinformed his readers when he said
the following:

> Friday was a singular day in our history: the first day in living mem-
> ory that Americans went to bed with fewer inalienable rights than
> they had when they woke up. Not just in living memory. Ever.

Tragically, there have been dozens of cases throughout our history
in which Americans had their most fundamental rights taken away.

The Alien and Sedition laws took away the right to criticize
elected officials, which was granted just a few years earlier by the
First Amendment. The Dred Scott case denied Black Americans the
right of citizenship, and even personhood. Several cases, during that
same period, denied Native Americans their fundamental rights.
Buck v. Bell authorized the sterilization of allegedly unfit citizens,
thus taking away their reproductive rights. In *Korematsu v. US*, more
than 100,000 American citizens of Japanese ethnicity were denied
the right to be free. In several cases during the McCarthy period,
Americans were denied the right to belong to the Communist Party.

In *Bowers v. Hardwick*, gay and lesbian Americans were denied the right to sexual freedom. Capital defendants were denied the right to life when the Supreme Court essentially reversed its decision outlawing capital punishment. At the beginning of the 20th century, many Americans were denied the right to be united with their families when racist immigration laws were enacted, limiting the number of ethnic minorities that were permitted to become citizens.

In addition to those rights, most of which today are recognized, many Americans over the years were denied rights that they deemed fundamental, such as the right to pray in schools, the right of Mormons to practice polygamy, property rights under the early New Deal, and the right to travel freely and not wear masks during the COVID-19 pandemic. The Violent Crime Control and Law Enforcement Act of 1994 severely limited the rights of defendants to habeas corpus. And now, many Americans, including Tribe himself, would severely curtail what many Americans believe is their Second Amendment right to "keep and bear Arms."

Tribe's blanket statement that never in history have Americans gone to bed with fewer rights than when they woke up is not only wrong historically and constitutionally, but also extremely insensitive to African Americans, Native Americans, the mentally ill, Japanese Americans, and other marginalized groups that have been denied the most basic rights over the years.

The truth, which Tribe denies in the interest of his partisan narrative, is that the pendulum of rights has swung widely throughout our history. Martin Luther King Jr.'s "arc of the moral universe" has not always pointed in the direction of rights—or justice. In a democracy with a complex system of separation of powers, checks and balances, and federalism, there will always be some back and forth with regard to rights. As Roger Baldwin, the founder of the American Civil Liberties Union, put it: "The struggle for liberty never stays won." So, too, with the eternal struggle for rights. Tribe seems to take for granted that his preferred rights are an ever-expanding given.

He is wrong. We must not assume that rights, once recognized, will never be taken away. We must persist in struggling to preserve them, through the courts, legislatures, executives, constitutional amendments, public opinion, and other lawful means.

No one benefits from false and ideologically driven history of the kind that Tribe and his ilk try to sell in reaction to this wrongful decision. Falsehoods will not set us free. Only hard work, based on truth, will push the arc toward justice.

Should protesters be allowed to shout in front of justices' homes?

Pro-abortion protestors have assembled in front of Justice Samuel Alito's family home in an obvious effort to intimidate or punish him. It will not undo the overruling of *Roe v. Wade*, but the question arises: are such protests legal and/or desirable?

As to the legality, there is a specific <u>statute</u> that criminalizes protest in front of the residences of judges, jurors, or witnesses, which are intended to interfere with or obstruct justice. While that statute might be constitutional as it related to efforts to influence the verdicts of jurors, the testimony of witnesses, or possibly even the decisions of elected judges during a trial, it is probably unconstitutional as applied to justices and appellate judges with lifetime appointments who are deemed to be immune from outside pressures.

The First Amendment protects the right to protest and assemble, which includes the right to object to any governmental action, including that of the judiciary. But it permits narrow and neutral time, place, and manner restrictions, such as decibel levels, reasonable distance requirements, and nighttime prohibitions. Accordingly, I would defend the constitutional rights of pro-abortion advocates to assemble peacefully, not too loudly, across the street from the home of a judge or a justice who is involved in rendering controversial decisions. Such restrictions must be the same for pro- and anti-abortion protesters—and for any others.

This does not mean that I personally approve of such tactics. I think it is wrong, as a matter of policy and decency, to disrupt the personal and family lives of justices and judges, even if one is strongly opposed to their decisions. Such advocates are free to protest in front of the Supreme Court, in front of Congress, and in front of the home of only one government official—namely, the president, who lives in the "people's house." I think interfering with the personal lives of judges, whether in their homes, the restaurants they eat in, or their children's schools, goes beyond what should be acceptable in a democracy. Such actions, even if constitutionally protected, should be condemned by decent people.

We live in an age where many, on both sides of the political spectrum, believe, and act on the belief that noble ends justify ignoble means. That of course is a matter of degree. There may well be extreme situations where such intrusive protests might, under some circumstances, be morally acceptable. But this should not apply to protesting unjust judicial decisions of a divided court. There are acceptable responses to perceived judicial injustices. These include protests in front of the appropriate institutions, congressional hearings, legislation, even constitutional amendments. They certainly include organizing voters to change the political dynamics that allow such injustices to occur.

Obviously, there is a continuum of protests being waged today, ranging from peaceful picketing in appropriate venues to violence of the sort that occurred in parts of the United States following the killing of George Floyd. Most nonviolent protests are constitutionally protected. Violent ones are not. And there are close cases that may turn on the specific facts, such as entering the Capitol to protest the counting of the votes of presidential electors. (I am representing one such defendant.)

There should be no confusion, however, between what is constitutionally permissible and what should be encouraged by decent people. I supported the right of Nazis to march through the streets of Skokie, despite the outrageous immorality of what they were doing. Accordingly, it is entirely appropriate for decent people—from the president to an average citizen—to object to the protests now being conducted in front of Alito's home. But this should not lead pundits who oppose such protests to argue, as some have done, that these ill-conceived protests are not constitutionally protected.

The First Amendment protects the right to be wrong, to be immoral, to be ill-mannered, and to go right up to the line where constitutionally protected advocacy can be made criminal. That line—unclear as it sometimes is—is important to preserve. It should not be tampered with by those who have strong feelings against intruding on the privacy of justices and judges.

Two related issues: first, judges and justices must be accorded all necessary protections against unlawful behavior, especially physical threats. Second, the same rules and levels of protection must apply to the right as to the left, to pro- as well as antiabortion protesters. The First Amendment does not pick political, ideological, or partisan sides. All advocacy is equally protected as a matter of constitutional law, if not as a matter of morality.

So, I will protest the morality of those who are demonstrating in front of Alito's home, while defending their right to do so peacefully and within constitutional limits.

Why don't we know who leaked the opinion overruling *Roe*?

Justice Samuel Alito recently stated that the leak of his draft opinion overruling *Roe v. Wade* had endangered the lives of justices by giving potential assassins a motive to change the vote by killing one or more of them. He also said that this leak had created distrust within the court.

In light of the seriousness of this breach, the question must be asked: why has the perpetrator not been identified and appropriately sanctioned? The first answer is obvious, the second not so much.

The first answer is that the Chief Justice assigned the Supreme Court Marshal's Office to do the investigation. I know that office. I clerked in the Supreme Court. I have had contact with them since. They are a great bunch of people, headed by a wonderful marshal. But they are <u>totally</u> unequipped to conduct an investigation of this magnitude. They do not have subpoena power, nor can they immunize witnesses to testify. The tools at their disposal are limited to questioning possible witnesses and asking to review telephone and computer records. That is not likely to produce any results. Everyone knows that whoever did this would have their legal careers seriously affected, if not ended. No one could trust a lawyer who engineered such a breach.

So, in light of the extreme unlikeliness that the Marshal's Office would be able to uncover the source or sources of this breach, why did the Chief Justice—a decent, thoughtful, and truthful man—assign the Marshal's Office to conduct this investigation?

This gets to the second question, whose answer is necessarily more speculative: is there a real desire within the Supreme Court to uncover the truth?

The most likely suspects in this dangerous breach are employees of the Court: law clerks, printers, and perhaps even justices. Guilt may well be a matter of degree. For example, if one law clerk knows that another law clerk did it and assisted in the cover-up, they would be guilty. The same would be true of a justice who knew but didn't come forward. Then there is the matter of suspicion short of actual evidence. Rumors are swirling around the high court as to who might be responsible.

Some people are pointing the finger at a pro-*Roe* law clerk who might have been motivated to engage in an act of civil disobedience in order to put pressure on a swing justice. Others point the finger at an anti-*Roe* law clerk who might have wanted to lock in a justice who might be having second thoughts. And then there is always the possibility that an employee—say, someone in the printing office—might have been the leaker. The least likely suspects would be the justices themselves, though it is not beyond the realm of possibilities that a justice might have implicitly encouraged a law clerk to do the deed.

Accordingly, it may not be in the interest of the Supreme Court as an institution to expose the malefactor. Right now, the situation is stable, despite Justice Alito's accusation and parade of horribles. Justice Alito did the right thing to call attention to the seriousness of the breach, but he could have gone further.

Justice Alito and others concerned about the dangers implicit in the breach should now be calling for an outside investigator with the power to issue subpoenas, grant immunity, and employ other traditional law enforcement tactics that are both constitutional and ethical. Congress has the power to legislate such a special investigator. The Justice Department may also have the power to appoint a special investigator, despite the uncertainty over whether the leaking of an unpublished Supreme Court opinion is a crime or merely a breach of rules and ethics. The integrity of the Supreme Court and the secrecy of its proceedings are essential aspects of governance. And the government has the power to determine who may have violated the rules, who may have covered up the violation, and who knew about it either before or after the fact.

Politico, the internet media to which the opinion was leaked, may well know the identity of the leaker. They claim to have checked the authenticity of the draft opinion before publishing it. They will, of course, claim journalistic privilege and refuse to identify their source, as is their right under the laws of most jurisdictions. They could be asked to describe their methodology of checking, which might provide a clue to the identity of the source. But that, too, might be protected, in at least some jurisdictions, as privileged journalistic methodology. Carefully targeted questioning may provide some unprivileged clues that could further the investigation.

One thing seems clear: without an outside investigator with the necessary tools, we will never get to the bottom of this mystery. What remains unclear is whether those currently in charge of the "investigation" are sufficiently motivated to rock the boat and possibly harm the institution of the Supreme Court by having the truth come out. But in a democracy, uncovering truth is more important than protecting institutions, even the Supreme Court. So, a special investigator should be appointed, and let the chips fall where they may. The American public should not be kept in the dark about one of the most important security breaches in American history.

CHAPTER 2

Guns, Death, and Crime

The Supreme Court's decision on gun control and the Second Amendment should be considered in the context of gun violence in the United States. I have written about these issues in several op-eds.

The NRA's anti-American narrative: no excuse for gun violence like the Uvalde school shooting

Anyone believing the nonsense spewed by speakers at the NRA convention in Houston—which coincided with the grieving over the Uvalde, Texas, school massacre—would come away with the impression that the United States is the most evil, deranged, and socially deviant nation in the world. The antiscience narrative being promoted by those who refuse to change America's permissive gun laws is that the easy availability of guns has absolutely no relationship to the high number of school shootings and other gun crimes that plague our nation.

According to the NRA parrots, the causes of gun violence are Americans who are evil, mentally ill, and socially maladjusted, and who just happen to use guns rather than knives or bats to perpetrate their mass killings. "Guns don't kill, people do," according to this mantra. If this were true, then it would follow, from the indisputable fact that the United States is among the world's leaders in gun-related violence and deaths, that we must also lead the world in people who are evil, mentally ill, and socially maladjusted. But the NRA, which boasts of its patriotism, would never come out directly and level such an un-American and demonstrably false accusation against the American people.

The truth, of course, is that Americans are not different enough as a people from the citizens of other democracies to explain why these nations have so many fewer gun crimes. There are evil people in all countries, but in our country these evil people are much more likely to use their easily available guns to do evil things to good people. The rates of mental illness and social maladjustment are not different enough in this country from those in Sweden, Ireland, Spain, or most of the rest of the world to explain the enormous difference in gun violence. The fact is that in our country more of these people use their easily available guns to commit mayhem against innocent victims.

There is only one variable that explains the dramatically higher rate of gun violence in the United States than in any comparable country. That variable is the easy availability of guns. No one has ever successfully challenged the direct correlation between gun availability and gun violence, and no one ever will.

The correlation is so clear and dramatic that it is impossible to deny causation. It cannot be mere coincidence that the nation with one of the highest levels of gun violence also boasts the highest level of gun availability. There is no escaping that lethal relationship. No amount of NRA blather about evil, mental illness, or social maladjustment can erase the fact that these constant phenomena—which are roughly equally spread out around comparable nations—cannot possibly be the variables that explain our vastly higher rates of gun violence. The relevant variable, as any honest social scientist will confirm, is the easy availability of guns.

It is possible, of course, that tightening the gun laws will not immediately reduce gun violence because there are so many guns out there and criminals will keep their guns regardless of the law. It is also possible that the easy availability of guns prevents some crimes. These are fair debates to have. So, too, with the reach of the Second

Amendment. What is not fair or honest is the phony attempt to deny the connection between the easy availability of guns and the high rate of gun violence, and to blame this American tragedy on factors that are not uniquely American.

It is important to assess the causes of gun violence honestly, even if the cures are not easily available. The first step to curing or reducing any problem is understanding its causes, even if they are multiple. Leaving out a major—in this case, THE major—cause of gun violence, because of political and partisan pressures, will make amelioration impossible. The reality is that people with guns they shouldn't have have killed and will continue killing innocent people, including many children.

The mass murderer in Uvalde was an obviously troubled eighteen-year-old who walked into a store and bought guns and rounds of ammunition capable of murdering hundreds of schoolchildren in a matter of minutes. It's hard to believe that it could have been worse, but it is clear that it could have been—and may be worse in some future tragedy. This mass murderer apparently had no mental assessment, waiting period, or any other of the many barriers to gun violence currently being proposed by reasonable Americans and being opposed by unreasonable ones.

Changing our gun laws to make it impossible for eighteen-year-olds like the mass murderer in Uvalde to buy semiautomatic or assault-style weapons and unlimited amounts of ammunition may not end school shootings. But such measures, along with other reasonable restrictions, can go a long way toward reducing the number of funerals of gun victims that have become all too common in our country.

Did the FBI have to kill the synagogue hostage taker?

Although not all the facts are known, the ones we do know raise the troubling question of why the FBI had to kill Malik Faisal Akram, the man who held four Jews hostage in the Texas synagogue. This is certainly not a popular question to ask, as we rightfully celebrate the heroic escape of the hostages, but it is an important one.

Based on what we now know, the three remaining hostages—one had been released earlier—had already scurried to safety before the FBI opened fire. If that is true, why didn't the FBI simply leave Akram alone and surrounded in the synagogue with no hostages for bargaining chips? Did he pose a danger to anyone at that point? Yes, he was armed, but a man with a loaded pistol surrounded by dozens of well-protected SWAT team members would not seem to pose a sufficient threat to warrant the use of lethal force when there were nonlethal alternatives. They could simply have waited him out at that point, until he fell asleep or became hungry. It is true that he might have killed himself—he said he would not emerge alive—but that would be no worse than what actually happened.

There may be good explanations for the course of action undertaken by the FBI. Maybe the SWAT team was unsure that all the hostages were safe at the moment when it made its first move. Perhaps the attack began before the hostages escaped. The "fog of war" applies to nighttime rescue operations, as it does to war. There are several related questions that should be asked: Who made the decision to breach the synagogue and go after the hostage-taker? Was it justified at the time it was made? Once the SWAT team was in the synagogue, did they have to use lethal force? Did the hostage-taker fire at them? Did he pose any other threat? These judgment calls had to be made quickly and under pressure. It is easy to Monday morning quarterback any such decision, and we should resist the temptation to do so, while at the same time asking questions that may be important for future hostage situations.

So, I am not judging or condemning the FBI. Nor am I defending Akram. What he did was indefensible, and he should have been killed if that were necessary to save the hostages. But was it?

It would have been far better for Akram to be taken alive, questioned, and put on trial, if that could have been done safely. The FBI might have learned about others who may have been complicit, or about other plots. They may also have learned how he was able to get into the US so easily.

But the fundamental issue transcends the benefits and costs of capture versus killing. As a nation, we are involved in a debate—some call it a "reckoning"—about the use of deadly force, especially as directed against racial minorities. Although this is not the typical case of police overreaction, it may bear on the more general issue.

So let all the facts be disclosed and serve as the basis for a discussion about the use of deadly force and its alternatives during hostage situations. All reasonable doubts should always be resolved in favor of protecting the hostages and against the hostage-taker. But there will be situations in which there are no such doubts—in which not using deadly force poses no risk to the hostages or the SWAT team. Was this one of those situations? Only a fair and open consideration of all the evidence will answer that pressing question.

The dangerous trend behind Officer Kim Potter's conviction

The jury's conviction of Minnesota police officer Kim Potter for the death of Daunte Wright, coupled with the judge's denial of bail pending her appeal, is a double injustice with dangerous implications for policing in America.

Officer Potter, a decorated policewoman with more than two decades of service, simply did not commit a crime. The prosecution conceded that she did not intend to shoot Wright and that she made a mistake by pulling out and firing a gun instead of a Taser.

Under American law, honest mistakes are not crimes—even if they result in tragic deaths. For example, an elderly driver accidentally putting a foot on the gas instead of the brake and killing a child is not necessarily a crime. It becomes a crime only if the action was reckless, involving a conscious decision to engage in conduct that the defendant knows poses a high risk of serious injury or death.

In this case, there was no evidence that Potter consciously made the decision to deploy and fire a gun as distinguished from a Taser. Nor was there sufficient evidence to demonstrate that Potter's conscious decision to stun Wright was criminal. Wright had an outstanding warrant for an armed crime, and his conscious decision to resist arrest and get back in his car constituted a direct threat to the life of Potter's fellow officers and others. She was right to stun him, but she made a mistake by firing the wrong weapon.

Even worse than the jury's verdict was the judge's decision to deny Potter bail pending appeal. There is a substantial likelihood that Potter's conviction will be reversed by an appellate court. Potter is neither a flight risk nor a danger to the community. The judge's decision to throw her into prison seems lawless and calculated to appease the public lust for holding police accountable, even in cases where the facts and the law do not justify imprisonment.

The conviction and imprisonment of Officer Potter represents a dangerous trend in American law. Prior to the racial "reckoning" that followed the unjustified killing of George Floyd by Minneapolis police officer Derek Chauvin in May 2020, a once-respected officer like Potter would never have been charged with criminal conduct for her tragic mistake. But the public demanded that she be charged. Indeed, some called for her to be accused of murder.

Elected prosecutors—and we are the only country I know of that elects prosecutors—often are more interested in pleasing the voters than in doing justice. This certainly seems to be the case here.

Every American, regardless of race or political persuasion, should be concerned when a decent police officer is indecently charged and convicted for making the kind of honest mistake that any person could make when confronted with the pressures of a life-or-death immediate decision. Police officers will be disincentivized by this decision to take actions that may be necessary to protect innocent life.

Only rarely do police officers actually fire their guns or their Tasers, but sometimes such action is necessary. When action is taken under circumstances such as those faced by Officer Potter, occasional honest mistakes are inevitable—and such mistakes could go both ways. What if Potter had failed to stop Wright and he had gotten back behind the driver's wheel and killed another officer as well as several pedestrians? That, too, would have been an honest mistake.

Criminal law is supposed to apply to bad people consciously making bad decisions, which they know or should know are in violation of the law. It should not apply to good police officers who make honest decisions that turn out to be wrong.

Potter should appeal her conviction and denial of bail. Not only should police organizations file briefs in her support; so should civil liberties groups like the American Civil Liberties Union, which should be concerned about the misapplication of the criminal law to satisfy voters.

The Minnesota appellate courts should carefully review the record in this case, including the evidence and the judge's instructions. The function of appellate courts is to be a step removed from the passions of the crowd and to apply the law neutrally and fairly. Such an application of the law to Officer Potter should result in an immediate decision to free her on bail, and then a subsequent decision to reverse her conviction, with instructions to dismiss the indictment.

Officer Potter is not a criminal. She did not commit a crime. She appeared devastated by her mistake, both at the time of the incident and when she testified in her own defense. Both justice and the rule of law require that she be set free.

Who's culpable for the Baldwin shooting?

The shooting of Halyna Hutchins is first and foremost a tragedy. It should never have happened. It resulted from cost- and corner-cutting. As a caring human being, I extend my warmest condolences to the Hutchins family.

As a criminal law professor for half a century, I am fascinated by this case. It is one I would have discussed in class and might well have given as an exam question.

In general, ordinary negligence is not a crime. For example, Minneapolis police officer Kim Potter's mistake of pulling out the wrong weapon—which resulted in her killing Daunte Wright—should never have been charged as a crime. And it wouldn't have been, if not for the George Floyd and other police killings.

So, what about the shooting of Halyna Hutchins? Under New Mexico law, negligent homicide by firing a gun is a petty misdemeanor. For it to rise to the level of a felony requires a higher level of culpability.

There is an easy question of culpability and a hard one in this case. The easy question is whether there is culpability as a general matter. The answer is clearly yes. The killing of Halyna Hutchins was a crime. It was the result of gross negligence and willful decisions to cut corners by hiring inexperienced—and as it turns out, incompetent—professionals, whose job it was to prevent just this sort of tragedy.

The hard question is who, if anybody, is criminally responsible? This may sound like a foolish question—if I am so sure there was a crime, how can I have any doubt about who the criminal is? But there is an enormous difference between concluding that criminal conduct occurred and being able to pinpoint a particular individual against whom guilt can be established beyond a reasonable doubt.

There is no presumption of innocence as to whether a death should be deemed criminal. The presumption of innocence attaches not to events, but to individuals. So, strange as it may seem, there can be a "crime" without there being a "criminal." That may well be the case here.

It will be exceedingly difficult, based on the evidence as we now know it, to prove beyond a reasonable doubt that Alec Baldwin is guilty of a crime. Yes, he had responsibilities as the last actor handling the gun and as one of the producers who oversees the entire enterprise. That may be enough for civil liability, but it will be difficult to prove criminal negligence because the person responsible for handing him the gun assured him that it was "cold."

So, the question then becomes, does the person who handed Baldwin the gun bear criminal responsibility for not checking it? That depends on that person's precise role, and what he or she did or didn't do.

Though several people may be charged together, this crime cannot be charged as a conspiracy, because there was probably no agreement, explicit or implicit, to allow a loaded gun on the set. Rather, the combined actions and inactions of a number of interrelated people brought about the tragedy.

The death of Brandon Lee in 1993 made clear that, when it comes to accidental shootings on movie sets, there is civil responsibility, and increased likelihood that one or more people would be charged with a crime. But the more recent case is not a slam dunk under New Mexico law. Nor would it be under the laws of most other jurisdictions.

The key question remains: how do we prevent this kind of utterly preventable tragedy from ever occurring again? I played an advisory role in the Brandon Lee case, and I thought its result—no criminal prosecution, but considerable civil liability—would change the realities on every movie set. That didn't happen, as evidenced by this tragedy. Will it now happen? Or will profits still be placed before safety?

There is one simple and obvious solution. Laws must be passed absolutely prohibiting the presence of any fireable weapon or any projectile capable of being fired from a weapon on any movie set. The Second Amendment is not for movie sets. Real guns have no place in the hands of actors. CGI technology has improved immeasurably since the Brandon Lee case. The firing of every gun in every movie must be filmed using CGI rather than gunpowder, blanks, or real guns. This should have been done immediately following the Brandon Lee case. It must be done now. No questions asked. Life is more important than making movies or saving a few dollars.

Let the preventable death of Halyna Hutchins serve to prevent future deaths on movie sets.

Chapter 3

Death in Ukraine: Can the Law Do Anything?

The Russian invasion of Ukraine has caused death and suffering among both civilians and soldiers. It is clearly an unlawful aggression under any reasonable interpretation of the law of war. Yet the deeply flawed and limited international legal system can do little to stop it or deter future illegal aggressions. In this chapter, I discuss why that is so.

Biden is wrong about genocide in Ukraine.
President Joe Biden used the word "genocide" to describe Russian President Vladimir Putin's war crimes in Ukraine. He is wrong—and to see why, let's go back nearly eighty years.

A sixteen-year-old girl named Maria Kostipolis is working as an apprentice to a dressmaker on the island of Rhodes, in Greece, in 1944. She is on the way to church, where she sings in the choir. She doesn't have any Jewish friends or relatives. Suddenly the Gestapo arrests her and her father. The accusation: that her father's father—now long dead—was a Jew before his family converted to Greek Orthodoxy when he was two years old. He was never told of his Jewish heritage.

The Gestapo had reviewed birth records going back a hundred years and determined that Maria and her father were genetically

Jewish, according to Nazi racial categorization. They were put on a ferry and then a train and arrived at Auschwitz four days later, where Maria was made to serve as a Reich prostitute for the camp guards. After three months, she was sent to the gas chamber, and her body was cremated.

There were many such "Marias"—the one described above is a composite of such victims—that were murdered by the Nazis, including nuns and priests with a Jewish grandparent. Nothing mattered to the Nazis other than genetics.

That is genocide. That was the Holocaust. That is the systematic attempt to exterminate every person in the world with Jewish genetic makeup, regardless of their religion, nationality, occupation, politics, or any other characteristics. No matter where they lived—no matter how far they were from the war or from land the Nazis wanted to clear for German expansion—if you were a genetic Jew, you were targeted for extermination. As Elie Wiesel put it: not every victim was a Jew, but every Jew was a victim. This was not part of the German war effort. To the contrary, it was inconsistent with any military goal. Soldiers were diverted from fighting the military enemy to the service of fighting the genetic enemy. Jews who could have helped Germany beat the United States in the race to develop an atomic bomb were gassed, shot, or escaped. Implementing the Nazi genocide—an entirely separate and often incompatible goal—was as important as prevailing on the battlefield. When Hitler and Goebbels committed suicide, they knew they had lost the military war, but they also knew they had won a significant victory in their war against the Jewish "race."

Now let's compare that genocide—the very term was coined to describe Hitler's intention to exterminate every Jew on the planet—to Vladimir Putin's horrible war against Ukraine, and the criminal tactics he and his generals are employing. Let's begin with Putin's war aims, his goals in invading Ukraine. His primary goals were to replace the government of Ukrainian President Volodymyr Zelenskyy with a pro-Russian regime to rule over the Ukrainian people. Another goal was to annex the eastern and southern parts of Ukraine and to build a land bridge from Russia to Crimea. His means included waging a ferocious war against what he believed was a militarily weak Ukrainian army and to demoralize the civilian population by causing enormous numbers of civilian deaths, including many children. Both the ends and the means constitute war crimes, but neither constitutes the very different crime of genocide.

Genocide requires a plan to exterminate a racial, religious, tribal, ethnic, or genetic group. It is different in kind from what Putin has been doing. The Ukrainians are similar in all the above respects to ethnic Russians. They are Slavs, mostly Eastern Orthodox. They speak similar languages, and many Ukrainians are fluent in Russian. They eat the same food, enjoy the same music, and share a common history and heritage. There are differences, of course, and Ukraine is a separate nation with a high degree of nationalism, as evidenced by recent events. But whatever else you can say about Putin's war crimes—and much can and should be said about them—they simply do not come within the definition of genocide.

A truly genocidal policy, as that employed by the Nazis, would not have allowed more than four million Ukrainians to escape. It would not have engaged in prisoner exchanges. It would have tried to exempt the millions of ethnic and linguistic Russians who live in Eastern Ukraine and who have suffered among the most horrendous brutalities.

It is important to keep genocide separate as a war crime from the serious crimes of waging aggressive war, targeting civilians, and the like. The memory of the Holocaust and of the handful of other genocides that occurred in the 20th century, including those against Armenians and ethnic groups in Africa, should not be diluted by describing other serious crimes as "genocide."

Why won't we impose a no-fly zone over Ukraine?

There is a simple answer to the question many Americans are asking: why not accept the Ukrainian request for a lifesaving no-fly zone to protect its civilians? The answer is simple and important: because the Russians have nuclear weapons. If the Russians did not have nuclear weapons, the United States and NATO would not only impose a no-fly zone, but they might also send troops to stop the

Russian massacre. But the understandable fear is that these defensive actions, reasonable as they would be, might well provoke a nuclear confrontation.

The lesson, therefore, is that any nuclear power can now blackmail the world into accepting any bullying aggression, without fear of military intervention. That is true not only of Russia, but North Korea, as well. The difference is that North Korea does not seem to have aggressive territorial ambitions other than preserving its hermit tyranny over its own people.

There would also seem to be a clear lesson here with regard to Iran. For Iran to obtain nuclear weapons, it would probably act more like Russia than like North Korea. It might use its nuclear blackmail to invade Saudi Arabia, the United Arab Emirates, and other oil-rich neighboring countries. It might also use its nuclear threat against Israel, despite Israel's possession of a significant nuclear deterrent. As a former president of Iran once put it: Israel is a "one bomb state," meaning it could be wiped out with one nuclear weapon. Even if Israel were to retaliate and use its nuclear arsenal against Tehran, the trade-off would be worth it, according to this former Iranian leader, because it would destroy the sole nation-state of the Jewish people. It is this kind of irrational, suicidal thinking that has led Israel to state categorically that it will never allow Iran to develop a nuclear bomb—period.

Now the United States is considering reentering into a deal with Iran that will make it possible for the mullahs to develop a nuclear arsenal, assisted by the infusion of billions of dollars and the end of sanctions. Anyone who doubts whether Iran will continue its efforts to develop a deliverable nuclear weapon is either a fool or a knave. As Elie Wiesel once put it: "Never rely on the promises of your friends, but always believe the threats of your enemies." For him, this was the lesson of the Holocaust. And he made that statement in the context of Iran's repeated genocidal threats.

A deal between the United States and Iran will make it even more difficult for Israel to take the unilateral military action that may be required to stop the development of Iran's nuclear arsenal. Israel, along with the United States, will continue to subvert Iran's

nuclear ambitions by sabotage, espionage, and one-off targeted killings. But these tactics may not be enough. Whatever deal Iran makes
on its nuclear program will not prevent it from cheating and lying, as
it has done for several decades.

The United States should be wary of entering a new deal that
would increase the likelihood of a nuclear-armed Iran. It is not clear,
as a matter of constitutional law, whether the president even has the
authority to make such a deal without the approval of the Senate.
The rest of the world regards the Iran deal as a "treaty," and the
US Constitution requires that all treaties must be ratified by a two-
thirds vote in the Senate. Both Presidents Obama and Biden have
interpreted the Constitution to permit the executive to circumvent
this requirement by calling it a mere executive "deal," rather than
a full treaty. That is legally dubious, although finding proper Article
III "standing" to bring such a constitutional challenge might prove
difficult.

In the meantime—and we always live in the "meantime"—the
Biden administration should be very cautious about what it agrees
to with Iran. It should assume the worst, and it should be prepared
to act on that assumption if it turns out—as it certainly will, in this
case—to be true.

Let us not allow Iran to become a bullying Russia. Let us learn the
lesson that Ukraine is now painfully learning about nuclear-armed
bullies. Peace requires that Iran never be allowed to develop nuclear
weapons—no matter what it takes.

Why did the Nobel Committee not give Zelenskyy the Peace Prize?

The Nobel Peace Prize is awarded every October to a living person who has fought for peace. The specific criteria listed in Alfred
Nobel's will are limited to advancing "fellowship among nations,"
helping to reduce "standing armies," and promoting "peace
conferences." But the Committee has broadened them to include
protection of the environment, promotion of free speech, and
other activities that oppose war. Zelenskyy would seem to meet
these broadened criteria.

Perhaps the Committee was reluctant to award a Peace Prize to a leader who is actually engaged in war—even a war of self-defense. Hopefully, the war will be over by next year.

The prize is awarded only to living recipients. The question is, will Zelenskyy still be alive next year? He himself has acknowledged that he is Russia's "number one target," and we know from tragic experience how Putin deals with his targets. They are poisoned, thrown out of windows, and killed in other brutal and sometimes subtle ways. If he survives, awarding him the Prize may save his life. It may make it just a little bit harder for Putin to incur the wrath of the entire world by murdering the holder of the Nobel Peace Prize.

Over the years, the Peace Prize has been awarded to the best of people, including Elie Wiesel, and to the worst of people, including Yasser Arafat. The Committee likes to say that its nomination is designed not only to award past actions, but also to influence the present and the future of peacemaking activities. No award could meet those criteria as effectively as the Peace Prize for Zelenskyy. Even if awarding Zelenskyy the Nobel Peace Prize fails to influence Putin's conduct, it will send a powerful message to a largely, but not completely, unified world.

The Nobel Peace Prize is not awarded by the United States, or by the European Union, or by NATO. It is a universal prize that has been awarded to people from the most disparate of nations and the most diverse political views. It would be difficult even for Putin to distort the award into an attack by the West, by imperialists, by capitalists, or by—to use his misnomer—Nazis. It would show him and his people how united so much of the world is against his increasing brutality.

In March of 2014, Putin himself was nominated for the Nobel Peace Prize. Hitler had been proposed in the 1930s. And other villains have been on long and short lists in the hope that their inclusion might influence their behavior. That has not worked. Neither did the selection of Yasser Arafat change his terrorist mindset or actions. What Putin is doing is pure evil with no justification. What Zelenskyy is doing and saying is mostly[1] good with every reason to

---

1 See p. 124.

encourage such actions by others. It is rare, at least since the end of the Second World War, to experience such a clash between evil and good. To be sure, there have been other massacres and even genocides, but the invasion of an entirely peaceful nation cannot go unrecognized by a committee whose agenda includes rewarding the past and influencing the future.

Zelenskyy may not be alive to accept the Prize next year. In that tragic case, it could be given to the Ukrainian people for the massive and costly resistance they are putting up to Russian aggression. An award that recognizes this collective heroism might well encourage even greater resistance by other nations threatened by naked aggression.

Accordingly, as an emeritus professor of public law who is eligible to make nominations, I plan to nominate Zelenskyy for next year's Nobel Peace Prize, despite my criticism of several things he said.[2]

Nazi symbols should not be worn by Ukrainian soldiers.

CNN recently conducted an interview with a Ukrainian military leader involved in defending Mariupol against Russian aggression. As expected, the military leader was glorified as a heroic soldier interested only in defending the lives of innocent civilians. During the interview, one could see proudly displayed on the soldier's chest a bright yellow and black symbol, the "Wolfsangel," which is reminiscent of the Nazi swastika. The symbol, which was used by several notorious Nazi SS divisions during World War II, is widely used today by neo-Nazi groups around the world.

The CNN correspondent interviewing the commander did not identify the symbol during the interview. Many viewers were unaware, therefore, that CNN was glorifying a leader of the Nazi AZOV regiment.

It is understandable that decent people want to see Mariupol defended by all means possible. But the truth—and historical memory—requires that we not ignore the role of neo-Nazis wearing Nazi symbols in the Ukrainian army. Putin is lying when he says that his

---

2 See p. 124.

invasions of Ukraine were designed to de-Nazify a country ruled by a Jewish president. But Ukraine is wrong in allowing a military unit to display Nazi symbols and to include in its leadership white supremacists and overt Nazis. At the very least, the public has the right to know who these military leaders are and what they stand for. The leadership of the AZOV Brigade acknowledges its neo-Nazi roots but claims that it has changed in recent years. Yet it refused to change its Nazi symbol because so many of its soldiers insist on maintaining this visual connection to Nazism.

Some will believe that the necessary and desirable end to saving Mariupol justifies any means. They are wrong. Nothing justifies making heroes out of Nazis and forgetting the disastrous role Ukrainian Nazis played in the mass murder of Jews and Romani people during the Second World War. Ukrainians didn't wait for the Nazi army to enter Lviv and other cities in order to murder much of its Jewish population. They conducted their own pogroms against Jews. Too many Ukrainians willingly served as guards in Nazi death camps. Too many Ukrainians were willingly complicit with Hitler's policy of exterminating the Jews of Ukraine. Too many Ukrainians participated in the Babi Yar massacre of 30,000 Jewish children and women. Some Ukrainians tried to help their Jewish neighbors, but most did not. This history cannot be ignored in evaluating the current role of Nazis in the Ukrainian army.

It is imperative that the Ukrainian government demand that no soldier wearing the uniform of Ukraine or carrying its flag be allowed to display Nazi symbols.

Defenders of the role of the AZOV regime in the Ukrainian army claim that all democratic armies contain some neo-Nazis. That is certainly true of Germany, France, and even the United States. But none of these countries—indeed, no country of which I am aware— allows its soldiers to display Nazi symbols on their uniforms and to proudly assert their support for elements of the Nazi ideology, including white supremacy. This must stop, regardless of the cost. There are moral red lines that cannot be crossed. One of them is Nazism. It will be argued that nothing can be done about this in the midst of a war for the survival of Ukraine. That is wrong. President Zelenskyy can issue an order demanding that no Nazi symbols be displayed on any Ukrainian uniform. That is the least he can do even if he can't purge his military of all Nazis, neo-Nazis, and Nazi sympathizers.

Unless Zelenskyy does this, or something like it, Ukraine's moral standing will suffer. Some will begin to believe Putin's lies about the "widespread" influence of Nazism in Ukraine. Others will wish a plague on both houses, if one of them includes Nazis and the other includes war criminals. Even in the midst of war, moral considerations must apply. Ukraine is demanding of the world that they put Russian war criminals on trial, and they are right in so demanding, because morality requires accountability. President Zelenskyy understandably demands that other countries place morality ahead of their narrow self-interest. Zelenskyy must demand that of his nation, as well. Morality requires that Ukraine, CNN, and others not make heroes out of Nazis, even Nazis who may perform some heroic acts. Some German Nazis during WW II also acted heroically—at least by their standards. But Nazism must never be tolerated, and certainly not glorified, if Zelenskyy's righteous call for "never again" is to be more than a cliché.

Has the Metropolitan Opera violated antidiscrimination laws by firing a Russian singer?

I had planned to see the Metropolitan Opera's production of *Turandot* starring Anna Netrebko. But the Met fired her on the ground that she is Russian and did not sufficiently condemn Vladimir Putin for waging war in Ukraine. She did condemn the war but refused to condemn Putin personally. If she had, she would be endangering her family, friends, and her own ability to ever return safely to her homeland. Netrebko is an Austrian citizen, but her country of origin is Russia.

The law of New York and many other jurisdictions prohibits employment discrimination based on national origin. Her firing would seem on its face illegal. Had she been born in the Donbas region of Ukraine instead of across the border in Russia, she would not have been fired even if she had refused to condemn the war or Putin. She would not have been asked her political views. But because she was born in Russia, her associations before the war with the leader of that country—she says she met him "only a handful of times"—were scrutinized, and she was required to take a disloyalty oath condemning him.

Here is what she said:

> I am opposed to this senseless war of aggression, and I am calling on Russia to end this war right now, to save all of us. We need peace right now.

She also wrote:

> I expressly condemn the war against Ukraine and my thoughts are with the victims of this war and their families.

But she refused to go further, insisting that:

> Forcing artists, or any public figure, to voice their political opinions in public and to denounce their homeland is not right. . . . I am not a political person. . . . I am an artist and my purpose is to unite people across political divides.

Netrebko's problem is that before the war, she did express political views: she supported Putin and pro-Russian Ukrainian separatists, though she has now expressed "regret that past statements of mine could have been misinterpreted."

Despite her rather tepid apology, Netrebko has lost work in Russia and is widely condemned by fellow Russians as a traitor during a time of war. As Simon Morrison, a Princeton music professor, aptly put it: "She's damned if she does, and damned if she doesn't."

Not every artist born in Russia can be expected to demonstrate the courage of my friend Evgeny Kissin, the great pianist, who did denounce Putin, the war, and the Russian Government. He will probably never set foot in his birthplace again—certainly not as long as Putin is in charge.

I agree with Netrebko that artists should not be required to express political views if they choose not to. Her case is a bit more complex because she chose to support Putin and pro-Russian separatists in the past, thus thrusting herself, even if only slightly, in contentious political issues. The lesson that other musicians will learn from Netrebko's dilemma is to use their voices to sing and not to take political positions that may come back to haunt them. It is a mixed lesson because we want artists to speak out—when we agree with what they are saying. But in this age of quickly changing criteria for cancellation, prudent artists will decline to express any potentially controversial views. It is too late for Netrebko to erase her prewar statements, so her cancellation by some organizations will probably persist, at least until the war is over.

Nonetheless, the Metropolitan Opera's decision to fire her, at least in part, because of her national origin may put my beloved opera company on the wrong side of antidiscrimination law. Her views would probably not have become the subject of political scrutiny if not for her national origin. And that may be enough to violate the antidiscrimination rules.

CHAPTER 4

Death in the Middle East: Can It Be Stopped?

The conflict in the Middle East—involving Israel, the Palestinian Authority, and Iran and its surrogates—has caused many deaths and threatens to cause many more. There are microissues, such as the death of a Palestinian journalist, macroissues, such as Iran's efforts at developing a nuclear arsenal. I have written extensively about these issues in my books and op-eds.

Who killed the Palestinian journalist?

The United States government has just concluded a forensic study of the shooting of Shireen Abu Akleh, the Palestinian American who worked for *Al Jazeera*. She was shot while covering an Israeli military action against terrorists who had murdered numerous Israeli civilians. While Israeli soldiers began trying to arrest terror suspects, Palestinians began to shoot at them. They returned fire, and in the process a bullet hit Shireen Abu Akleh and she died.

The American investigation came to three conclusions: (1) that because the bullet was deformed by hitting the journalist's helmet, it was forensically impossible to determine whether it had been shot from an Israeli or Palestinian gun; (2) that circumstantial evidence, including the location of shooters, suggests that it is "likely," but far from certain, that the bullet probably came from an Israeli soldier;

and (3) that the evidence overwhelmingly shows that no one targeted Shireen Abu Akleh, but rather that her death was a tragic accident resulting from the exchange of fire.

The Israelis now seem to accept these conclusions. The Palestinians persist in their totally unfounded and counterevidentiary claim that Israeli soldiers were ordered to target Shireen Abu Akleh because of her anti-Israel reporting. They also falsely claim that this is part of a policy of Israeli targeting of unfriendly journalists. Nothing could be further from the truth. These are completely fabricated, propagandistic claims that bear no relationship to reality. But the Palestinian Authority leadership will stop at nothing to put all the blame for everything on Israel, its leaders, and its soldiers.

Israeli leaders assert that even if the bullet had come from an Israeli soldier, the moral and legal blame lies squarely with the Palestinian groups who initiated the encounter: first, by encouraging terrorism against Israeli citizens, and second, by shooting at Israeli soldiers who were engaged in a completely lawful effort to arrest murderers.

The important point is that all the evidence must be disclosed so that the public can decide for itself how to allocate responsibility for this tragedy.

Another important point is to put the killing of this one journalist in the context of the dozens of journalists who are killed each year covering military conflicts, such as those who have died in Ukraine.

When put in this context, it becomes clear that the international focus on this one shooting is nothing less than a manifestation of international anti-Semitism against the nation-state of the Jewish people. Whenever Israel does anything wrong, questionable, or sometimes even justifiable, the international community and the media tend to focus unprecedented attention on the only nation-state of the Jewish people. By comparison, the killings of other journalists are either ignored or buried.

At least until all the evidence is disclosed to the public, the book should be closed on the tragic death of Shireen Abu Akleh. Efforts by Palestinians leaders to bring this singular tragedy to the International Criminal Court violate the rules of that court, as well as the broader rules of international law. This was a tragedy, not a crime. And a tragedy should not be criminalized for political purposes. Hopefully, the Israeli military will augment Israel's already-cautious rules of engagement. But crucially, the Palestinian leadership must do more to discourage terrorism against innocent Israeli civilians. Unless that is done, more civilians and journalists will die.

President Joe Biden traveled to the Middle East in July 2022, where he met Israeli and Palestinian leaders. He had hoped that this issue would have been resolved to the satisfaction of both sides by the time he arrived there. But the Palestinians insisted on using the death of Shireen Abu Akleh to keep the issue of Israeli culpability alive. That is what the Palestinian leadership does, and what it has been doing for decades: using the tragic death of its "martyrs" to score political points. President Biden should discourage this gruesome tactic, which only produces more death and tragedy. That would be an appropriate memorial to the life and death of an important journalist.

New York Times pits "principle" against powerful "rabbis" in Iron Dome vote

In purporting to "report"—not editorialize—about why Alexandria Ocasio-Cortez (AOC) changed her vote from "no" to "present" on the Iron Dome funding, *New York Times* congressional correspondent Catie Edmondson "reported" the following:

"[Progressives] have been caught between their principles and the still powerful pro-Israel voices in their party, such as influential lobbyists and rabbis."

She cited no support for her "reporting" on the pressure placed by "powerful . . . rabbis," nor did she name them, because her "reporting" simply wasn't true. She just made it up, because it supported the anti-Semitic narrative that AOC and her Squad deploy to deflect legitimate criticism of their anti-Israel votes.

No powerful rabbis or lobbyists were needed to pressure the nearly five hundred Democrats and Republicans who voted to fund the Iron Dome defense system that was jointly developed by the United States and Israel and that is currently being used to defend American troops from rocket attacks. The Iron Dome kills no one. It saves the lives of Israeli Jews, Muslims, and Christians who are targeted by Hamas rockets. No objective person should oppose funding for this life-saving system. But Edmondson decided to "report"—make up—a canard that has deep roots in the sordid history of anti-Semitism: namely, that powerful rabbis—sometimes called "the elders of Zion"—pressured elected officials to surrender their patriotic American "principles" by voting in an unprincipled way in support of a foreign power. This not only demeans Jews as having dual loyalty, but it also insults every member of Congress who voted for this allegedly "unprincipled" result, presumably because of illicit pressure from lobbyists and rabbis, and not because they believed it was the right thing to do for America and its ally. No mention was made of powerful pro-Palestinian lobbyists or Imams, or of the pressure placed on AOC and others by radical leftists who hate Israel. No: it was "principles" that motivated the anti-Israel votes, and "powerful" rabbinical pressures that determined the "yes" and "present" votes. And this purports to be objective "reporting" from the newspaper of record.

After much criticism, the *Times* quietly removed the reference to "rabbis" without apologizing for its reporter's mendacious anti-Semitism or disciplining her for her journalistic malpractice. Just imagine how quickly a journalist would be canceled if she engaged in comparable bigotry toward another group. But the *Times* has long suffered from a double standard toward Jews and the Jewish nation.

The *Times* has repeatedly felt the need to apologize for its persistent insensitivity—and worse—toward Israel and its Jewish supporters. Remember the *Der Strummer*-like cartoon it published in its international edition. It must do better. It must take steps to identify and control biased reporters, such as Edmondson, and reporting, such as her false claim about powerful rabbis, before they have to apologize for the damage that has already been done.

The *Times* has the right to editorialize against Israel, as it constantly does. It has the right to publish multiple columns and op-eds that are skewed against Israel, while employing only one pro-Israel columnist. But it has no journalistic right to editorialize on its news pages, as it repeatedly does. It defrauds its readers by disguising its subjective and biased opinions as objective unbiased reporting of the news. In this regard, the *Times* is among the worst offenders of any influential newspaper.

So let the reader beware. You are not getting "all the news that's fit to print" about Israel.

You are getting only the "news" that its reporters and editors fit into their preconceived and biased narrative.

I challenge the Columbia School of Journalism, or any other objective academic institution, to conduct a study of the *Times* "reporting" on the Israeli-Palestinian conflict over the last few years. The results will shame the *Times* and caution its readers to skeptically evaluate what passes as "reporting."

In the meantime, the *Times* must publicly, clearly, and substantively apologize for its reporter lying about "powerful . . . rabbis" and explain how its editors could permit such an obviously anti-Semitic canard to be published in its pages. Quietly eliminating the offending words from its online version is cowardly and insufficient. It must acknowledge the harm that its false reporting has caused.

Is the Iran deal a treaty?

As negotiations continue as to whether the United States should reenter the so-called the Joint Comprehensive Plan of Action (JCPOA)—colloquially called the Iran "Deal"—the question arises: Is this agreement among nations a treaty? If it is a treaty, the Constitution requires that it be approved by two-thirds of the Senate. This is important because it is unlikely that the original Iran Deal or its proposed reentry by the United States could get two-thirds approval by the Senate. Nor is it clear that it could even get majority approval.

The Constitution, although it sets out a procedure for approving treaties, nowhere defines what a treaty is. The Framers would almost certainly have regarded a binding contractual obligation among multiple nations as a treaty. Indeed, several such treaties were approved by the Senate in the early days of our Republic.

In recent years, however, executives have circumvented constitutional constraints on foreign policy by simply renaming actions that presidents have taken. The Constitution requires that only Congress can declare war, but since the end of the Second World War, which was declared by Congress, presidents have engaged in warlike military actions without an explicit declaration by Congress. Likewise, presidents have entered into treaty-like agreements with foreign countries without seeking the two-thirds approval of the Senate. Such circumventions of the Constitution over time do not make them right as a matter of constitutional law. The Framers clearly intended to divide the war-making and treaty-making authority of the United States between the executive and legislative branches. That is part of our system of checks and balances.

President Barak Obama violated not only the spirit of the Constitution, but in my view its letter, by refusing to submit the Iran agreement to the Senate. The result of this failure was that President Donald Trump was able to rescind America's agreement to this deal by his own unilateral presidential declaration.

Now President Joseph Biden wants to reenter the Joint Comprehensive Plan of Action, and he wants to do it without Senate approval. I believe that there is a strong case for this action being unconstitutional. But that doesn't necessarily mean that the courts will strike down this presidential agreement, were it to be made. There are two constitutional doctrines that might prevent an unconstitutional agreement from being declared unconstitutional by the Supreme Court. The first is "standing": who would have the power to challenge such an agreement, which was not approved by the Senate, in court? Probably not an ordinary citizen, but perhaps a senator, or even more likely a group of senators, exceeding one third of the current Senate. They could claim that their constitutional powers had been abrogated by the president's unilateral action.

The second barrier might be the "political question" doctrine, pursuant to which the Supreme Court generally refuses to enter the political thicket over controversial and highly partisan issues. But the Supreme Court, over the past half-century, has entered into that thicket on numerous occasions, the reapportionment cases being the most obvious such example. Nothing could be more political than state legislative decisions about how to draw districts to favor one political party over the other, and yet the Supreme Court has jumped headlong into that thicket.

It is uncertain whether the current justices would take a case challenging the authority of the president to enter into multinational agreements, without the approval of the Senate. There are probably some justices who would argue that if it quacks like a treaty, looks like a treaty, acts like a treaty, then it must be ratified by two-thirds of the Senate without regard to what the president calls it. I'm reminded of the encounter between American journalist Theodore White and Chinese leader Mao, who invited him to dinner and served a stuffed pig. White, who was Jewish, said he couldn't eat pig. Mao then said that in China, the leader decides everything, and so he declared the pig to be a duck! Well, this isn't China, and the president alone does not get to decide that a "treaty" is a "deal" not requiring senate approval.

But even if the High Court were to duck this issue, the president and members of Congress are all sworn to follow the Constitution. Accordingly, I call on the president to submit this question to the Office of Legal Counsel and for that office to publish its conclusion. I also call on the Senate to hold hearings on the constitutionality of the president signing a deal that is really a treaty that should require Senate approval. The American public has a right to hear all sides of this controversial issue.

Why is the flawed Palestinian cause so prominent on the hard left?

The anti-Israel claims of the Palestinians, though deeply flawed, have become a central part of hard-left ideology, especially among those who adhere to so-called intersectionality. Why does the Palestinian cause get so much attention, when there are much more compelling causes around the world such as those of the Kurds, Uyghurs, and other stateless and/or oppressed people? There are more demonstrations on university campuses against Israel than against Russia, China, Belarus, and Iran! Why? The answer has little to do with the Palestinians, and everything to do with Israel, as the nation-state of the Jewish people. It is a political manifestation of international anti-Semitism. It is only because the nation accused of oppressing Palestinians is Israel.

This is not to say that is wrong to support the Palestinian cause. It is to say that it is wrong—and bigoted—to prioritize that deeply flawed cause over other, more deserving, causes. Not only does the hard left prioritize the Palestinians; it largely ignores other causes, just because Israel is on the other side of the Palestinian issue. The reality is as simple as that. It has little to do with the merits and everything to do with anti-Semitism. It calls itself anti-Zionism, but it is only a cover for anti-Jewish bigotry.

A recent example is the decision of Ben and Jerry's ice cream to boycott parts of Israel, while continuing to sell to countries in which far greater abuses occur. When asked why Ben and Jerry limit their boycott only to Israel, its founders admitted they had no idea. Well, I have an idea! In Ben and Jerry's case, their ignorant founders are simply useful idiots, following unquestioningly the crowd of hard-left anti-Semites. To paraphrase an old expression: bigot sees, bigot does.

But who is leading the crowd of anti-Semitic bigots? The movement to single out the nation-state of Israel for boycott, known as BDS, was originated by a Palestinian radical named Omar Barghouti, who doesn't hide the fact that his goal is the destruction of Israel and the substitution of a Palestinian state "from the river to the sea," meaning the Jordan river and the Mediterranean Sea—namely, all of current Israel. He and others who lead the BDS movement want to see this entire area *judenrein*, that is, ethnically cleansed of the more than seven million Jews who now "occupy" Muslim and Arab land. These "occupiers" include Jews who are Black and Brown; European, Asian, African, and American; and descendants of people who have lived there since before Islam began, and certainly before many current "Palestinians" moved there from Egypt, Syria, Lebanon, the Gulf, and North Africa. Jews are as indigenous to Israel as descendants of immigrants are to America.

Do the Palestinians deserve a state? Yes, but no more so than the Kurds and other stateless people. Why no more so? Because the Palestinians have been offered statehood numerous times and have rejected it. As the former leader of the Palestinian people put it when the two-state solution was first proposed in the late 1930s: "We want there not to be Jewish state more than we want there to be a Palestinian state."

This leader, Mohammed Amin al-Husseini, allied himself and his people with Nazi Germany during World War II. Al-Husseini spent the war years in Berlin with Hitler planning to bring the final solution to the Jews of what is now Israel. He was declared a Nazi war criminal. Yet his picture was featured in many Palestinian Arab homes, and he was regarded as a hero and leader.

Despite being on the losing side of the war, the Palestinians were offered a state on the vast majority of arable land, as part of a United Nations proposed two-state solution in which the Jews were offered a state on a far smaller area of arable land on which they were a majority. The Jews accepted the compromise two-state solution. The Arabs rejected it and went to war against the new Jewish state seeking to destroy it. It was this act of unlawful military aggression that resulted in the Palestinian refugee situation, which they call the "Nakba," the catastrophe. But it was a self-induced catastrophe. And many current Palestinian leaders and followers fault their predecessors for not accepting the two-state solution offered by the United Nations seventy-five years ago.

Rather than trying to negotiate for a state during the subsequent years, the Palestinian leadership under Yasser Arafat opted for terrorism against Israeli and international civilian targets. They could have had a state in 1948, 1967, 2000–2001, 2005, and 2008. They still preferred no Jewish state to a Palestinian state living in peace with Israel. They can have a state now, if they would negotiate a compromise instead of fomenting terrorism.

I wonder how many of those who demonstrate against Israel have any idea of this history. Or are they merely serving as useful idiots to those who know the history but want to undo it because it resulted in a nation-state for the Jewish people? It doesn't really matter. The bottom line is that the hard left's irrational opposition to Israel is a modern manifestation of the world's oldest and most enduring bigotry.

Banning Zionist—and only Zionist—speakers is a form of anti-Semitism.

Do clubs officially sponsored by the University of California at Berkeley School of Law have "Zionist-free zones," reminiscent of the early twentieth-century signs that reportedly said, "No Jews or dogs allowed"? Or are these clubs merely exercising their First Amendment rights by banning all Zionist speakers and only Zionist speakers? This is the question that is roiling not only the UC Berkeley campus, but campuses all across the country that see the answer setting a precedent for them.

Let us begin with the undisputed facts.

These clubs have amended their charters to disallow all Zionist speakers—even if they also support Palestinian rights and other progressive causes, and even if they intend to speak on a subject unrelated to Israel. If they are Zionists, they are not welcome to speak at these clubs about anything!

The alleged justification for this total ban on all Zionists—that is, people who believe that Israel has a right to exist—is to protect the *safety* and welfare of Palestinian students. This is patent nonsense. No students have been physically threatened by Zionists, and no student is entitled to be protected from ideas.

These clubs include the Berkeley Law Muslim Student Association, Middle Eastern and North African Law Students Association, Women of Color Collective, Asian Pacific American Law Students Association, Queer Caucus, Community Defense Project, Women of Berkeley Law, and Law Students of African Descent.

In other words, even Muslims, gays, feminists, and supporters of progressive causes seem to be excluded if they also believe Israel has the right to exist. By excluding ALL Zionists, the ban seems to cover Jews who favor a two-state solution, a return to the 1967 lines, and a right of return for all Palestinians.

Those clubs are engaging in a combination of Stalinism and anti-Semitism: Stalinism in the sense that they allow no dissenting views from their "politically correct" doctrine of no Israel; anti-Semitism in the sense that among all the nations of the world that are involved in controversies—Russia, Iran, China, Belarus, to name a few—they have singled out for banning only the nation-state of the Jewish people.

Imagine if a university club were to exclude all speakers who support Black Lives Matter. The current ban is even worse because it seems to ban all Zionist speakers—regardless of their views—from organizations that have nothing to do with Israel. A Jewish feminist could not speak to the women of UC Berkeley about abortion if it were discovered that she is a Zionist. That is pure bigotry.

The University of California at Berkeley is a public institution. If it in any way supports these organizations—financially or by allowing them to have offices on the campus—then it is effectively the State of California that is enacting and enforcing these bans. This constitutes state action and is governed by the First Amendment. The question is which way the First Amendment cuts. Does it give the clubs the right to exclude all speakers who are Zionists? Or does it prohibit state actors from demanding that all speakers disavow Zionism as a condition to exercising their First Amendment right to speak? And what about the rights of their potential audience members to hear them? The answers may also implicate federal funding for the university.

Clubs and universities generally have a right to choose their speakers, but there is a vast difference between individually deciding who will speak and making a collective decision banning all people of a particular ideology, religion, or race. This is particularly so when the ideology serves as a mask for anti-Semitism. Not all Jews are Zionists. Not all support Israel. Many, including me, disagree with some of Israel's policies, just as I disagree with some policies of every country, including the United States. Not all African Americans support Black Lives Matter, but enough do so that such a ban would constitute racial discrimination, just as a ban on all Zionists constitutes anti-Semitism.

These clubs are effectively banning most Jews. The dean of UC Berkeley School of Law implicitly made this point when he said that 90 percent of Berkeley's Jews, including him, would be banned by such a policy. This is discrimination pure and simple. The dean also said that he would discipline any club that actually discriminated on religion or "viewpoint" grounds. I hereby volunteer to present the case for Israel—or for gay marriage—at any or all of these clubs. It will be interesting to see if they exclude me—a proud, if sometimes critical, Jewish Zionist.

Although the current ban is only for speakers, its "logic"—protecting the safety of Palestinian—would extend to membership, even presence, at these clubs.

The dean also said that school policy prohibits discrimination in membership based on religion or point of view. This would seem to conflict with the "safety" rationale for the ban.

The ban is, sadly, also akin to a "loyalty oath" of the kind imposed by McCarthyites in the 1950s and opposed back then by the liberals and civil libertarians. Today's liberals and civil libertarians should strongly oppose these ideological tests, as well. But because they come from the intersectionalist left, many are silent, while others are complicit.

Kudos to the dean for condemning this bigotry, even while he defends their constitutional right to practice it. I have offered to publicly debate or discuss our different views of how the First Amendment impacts this ban.

Universities have an educational and moral duty to foster dialogue and learning, not banning and censorship. Public universities have a constitutional obligation to prohibit religious and ethnic discrimination. Berkeley is failing both tests.

The question remains: is their failure protected or prohibited by the First Amendment?

CHAPTER 5

Is the Death Penalty Cruel
and Unusual Punishment?

———————

"Just as death is different," so is the death penalty, as the Supreme
Court has said when dealing with the unique sentence of capital
punishment. The issue of whether to take life for life has plagued
humankind from the beginning of recorded history. The first biblical
reference to the death penalty occurs in the book of Genesis, when
God prohibits the killing of the murderer Cain. Soon thereafter God
tells Noah that he who sheds human blood shall by humans have his
blood be shed. The Ten Commandments prohibit murder, and the
subsequent laws of the Bible authorize the death penalty for a variety
of crimes, ranging from murder to being a stubborn child. But the
procedural safeguards required before a person could be put to death
were so stringent that the Talmud characterizes a court that sentenced
even one person to death over a seventy-year period as a bloody
court. By this standard, American courts are bloody indeed. Many
Americans have been executed and now face execution on America's
death rows. Only a portion of these will actually die at the hands of
the state, since appellate reversal is far more common in capital cases
than in cases involving imprisonment, because most courts recognize
that death, being irreversible is different from imprisonment.

The advent of DNA testing has disclosed many instances of
wrongful conviction. DNA is useful only in a limited number of

cases. Many capital cases involve only eyewitnesses and circumstantial inferences. People have been put to death on the basis of one eyewitness, despite their plausible claims of innocence. But the execution of the innocent is not the only reason for concern about the death penalty. It has been imposed unfairly, especially against the poor and disenfranchised. Few on death row have received zealous representation from competent counsel. The racial injustice permeates the death-penalty process.

Since I was a high school student, I have strongly opposed the death penalty. I came of age as Julius and Ethel Rosenberg were being executed. A relative of mine was the chaplain who sought to comfort them at their death. In high school I debated against the death penalty. I still have my debate note cards on which I argued that "it is possible that mistakes have been made" and it is better that one hundred murderers go to prison "than one innocent man go mistakenly to the electric chair." In law school I wrote letters to the editor calling for its abolition. I even opposed the execution of Adolf Eichmann, the man responsible for the death of millions of Jews.

When I became a law clerk for Justice Goldberg on the United State Supreme Court, the justice asked me to write a memorandum arguing that the death penalty was cruel and unusual punishment prohibited by the Eighth Amendment to our Constitution. He then asked me to show it to Justice William Brennan and to try to persuade him of our argument. I tell this story in the pages ahead. (The memorandum, written by a twenty-four-year-old, is published in Appendix A.)

The first substantive conversation I ever had with Justice Brennan was about the death penalty. I had just arrived at the Supreme Court as a clerk to Justice Arthur J. Goldberg. My initial assignment was to write a memorandum on the possible unconstitutionality of the death penalty. I set to work but found no suggestion in the case law that any court had ever considered the death penalty to be of questionable constitutionality. Just five years earlier, Chief Justice Earl Warren had written in *Trop v. Dulles* (1958) that "whatever the arguments may be against capital punishment, both on moral grounds and in terms of accomplishing the purposes of punishment—and they are forceful—the death penalty has been employed throughout our history, and, in a day when it is still widely accepted, it cannot be said to violate the constitutional concept of cruelty."

I duly reported this to Justice Goldberg, suggesting that if even the liberal chief justice believed that the death penalty was constitutional, what chance did he have of getting a serious hearing for his view that the cruel and unusual punishment clause should now be construed to prohibit the imposition of capital punishment? Justice Goldberg asked me to talk to Justice Brennan and see what his views were. Unless Justice Brennan agreed to join, the entire project would have to be scuttled, since Justice Goldberg, the Court's rookie, did not want to "be out there alone," against the chief justice and the rest of the Court.

I had previously met Justice Brennan several times over the preceding few years, since his son, Bill, was my classmate and moot-court partner at Yale Law School. I had also had lunch several times with the justice and his friend Judge David Bazelon, for whom I had clerked the previous year. But none of our discussions had been substantive, and I nervously anticipated the task of discussing an important issue with one of my judicial heroes.

I brought a rough draft of the memorandum I was working on to the meeting, but Justice Brennan did not want to look at it then. He asked me to describe the results of my research to him, promising to read the memorandum later. I stated the nascent constitutional case against the death penalty as best I could. I told him that the Supreme Court case law, especially the Court's 1910 decision in *Weems v. United States*, could be read as recognizing the following tests for whether a punishment was "cruel and unusual": (1) Giving full weight to reasonable legislative findings, a punishment is cruel and unusual if a less severe one can as effectively achieve the permissible ends of punishment (that is, deterrence, isolation, rehabilitation, or whatever the contemporary society considers the permissible objectives of punishment); (2) Regardless of its effectiveness in achieving the permissible ends of punishment, a punishment is cruel and unusual if it offends the contemporary sense of decency (for example, torture); and (3) Regardless of its effectiveness in achieving the permissible ends of punishment, a punishment is cruel and unusual if the evil it produces is disproportionately higher than the harm it seeks to prevent (for example, the death penalty for economic crimes).

In addition to these abstract formulations, I also told Justice Brennan that our research had disclosed a widespread pattern of unequal application of the death penalty on racial grounds. I cited national prison statistics showing that between 1937 and 1951, 233 Blacks were executed for rape in the United States, while only 26 whites were executed for that crime.

Justice Brennan encouraged me to continue my research, without making any promise that he would join any action by Justice Goldberg. Several weeks later, Justice Goldberg told me that Justice Brennan had agreed to join a short dissent from the denial of certiorari in *Rudolph v. Alabama* (1963)—a case involving imposition of the death penalty on a Black man who was convicted of raping a white woman. Justice William O. Douglas signed on, as well. The dissenters invited the bar to address the following questions, which they deemed "relevant and worthy of argument and consideration":

1. In light of the trend both in the country and throughout the world against punishing rape by death, does the imposition of the death penalty by those States which retain it for rape violate "evolving standards of decency that mark the progress of [our] maturing society," or "standards of decency more or less universally accepted"?

2. Is the taking of human life to protect a value other than human life consistent with the constitutional proscription against "punishments which by their excessive . . . severity are greatly disproportioned to the offenses charged"?

3. Can the permissible aims of punishment (e.g., deterrence, isolation, rehabilitation) be achieved as effectively by punishing rape less severely than by death (e.g., by life imprisonment); if so, does the imposition of the death penalty for rape constitute "unnecessary cruelty"?

As soon as the dissent was published, there was an immediate reaction. Conservative journalists had a field day lambasting the very notion that a court could strike down as unconstitutional a long-standing punishment that is explicitly referred to in the Constitution. One extreme criticism appeared in the *New Hampshire Union Leader* under the banner headline "U.S. Supreme Court Trio Encourages Rape":

> In a decision handed down last week three U.S. Supreme Court justices, Goldberg, Brennan, Douglas, raised the question of whether it was proper to condemn a man to death for the crime of rape if there has been no endangering of the life of the victim. This incredible opinion, of course, can serve only to encourage would-be rapists. These fiends, freed from the fear of the death penalty and knowing the saccharin sentimentality of many parole boards, will figure the penalty for their foul deed will not be too serious and, therefore, they will be inclined to take a chance.
>
> Thus, not content with forbidding our school children to pray in school, not content with banishing Bible reading from our schools, and not content with letting every type of filthy book be published, at least three members of the Supreme Court are now out to encourage rape.

Several state courts went out of their way to announce their rejection of the principle inherent in the dissenting opinion. This is what the Georgia Supreme Court said:

> With all due respect to the dissenting Justices, we would question the judicial right of any American judge to construe the American Constitution contrary to its apparent meaning, the American history of the clause, and its construction by American courts, simply because the numerous nations and States have abandoned capital punishment for rape. First, we believe the history of no nation will show the high values of woman's virtue and purity that America has shown. We would regret to see the day when this freedom loving country would lower out respect for womanhood or lessen her

legal protection for no better reason than that many or even all other countries have done so. She is entitled to every legal protection of her body, her decency, her purity and good name.

There was scholarly criticism, as well. In the *Harvard Law Review*, Professor Herbert Packer of Stanford wrote:

> In an interesting development, some members of the Supreme Court appear disposed to employ [recent constructions of the "cruel and unusual punishments" clause] to regulate the appropriate relation between crime and punishment. Three Justices recently noted their dissent from a denial of certiorari in terms that invite speculation about the role of constitutional adjudication in solving the age-old problem of whether and how the punishment may be made to fit the crime. . . . [However,] [s]ympathy with the legislative goal of limiting or abolishing the death penalty should not be allowed to obscure the difficulties of taking a judicial step toward that goal on the theory outlined by Justice Goldberg [in *Rudolph v. Alabama*]. . . . If one may venture a guess, what Justice Goldberg may really be troubled about is not the death penalty for rape but the death penalty. The problem may not be one of proportionality but of mode of punishment, the problem which concerned the framers of the eighth amendment and to which its provisions still seem most relevant. The Supreme Court is obviously not about to declare that the death penalty *simpliciter* is so cruel and unusual as to be constitutionally intolerable. Other social forces will have to work us closer than we are now to the point at which a judicial *coup de grâce* becomes more than mere fiat. Meanwhile, there may well be legitimate devices for judicial control of the administration of the death penalty. The burden of this Comment is simply that the device proposed by Justice Goldberg is not one of them.

These were the short-term reactions. Far more important, however, was the long-term reaction of the bar, especially the American Civil Liberties Union and the NAACP, which combined forces to establish a death penalty litigation project designed to take up the challenge of the dissenting opinion in *Rudolph*.

The history of this project has been recounted brilliantly by Professor Michael Meltsner in his book *Cruel and Unusual*, and I could not possibly improve upon it here. But the results achieved were dramatic. Meltsner and the other members of the Legal Defense Fund, a group that included a number of talented and committed lawyers, litigated hundreds of cases on behalf of defendants sentenced to death and, in many of these cases, succeeded in holding the executioner at bay until the Supreme Court was ready to consider the constitutionality of the death penalty.

The strategy was simple in outline: The Supreme Court should not be allowed the luxury of deciding the issue of capital punishment as an abstraction; instead, it must be confronted with the concrete responsibility of determining the immediate fates of many hundreds of condemned persons at the same time. In this way, the Court could not evade the issue, or lightly refuse to decide it, if the Court's refusal would result in the specter of mass executions of hundreds of convicts. However, the Court could decline to decide the ultimate issue—the constitutionality of capital punishment—if in doing so it could find some other way of keeping alive those on death row. And the litigants always provided the Court with this other way—a narrower issue, usually in the form of an irregularity in the procedure by which the death penalty was imposed or administered.

Thus, in the late 1960s, the Supreme Court decided a number of cases involving the administration of the death penalty; in each of these cases the Court declined to consider the ultimate issue, but it always ruled in favor of the doomed, thereby sparing their lives—at least for the moment. With the passage of each year, the number of those on death row increased, and the stakes grew higher and higher.

Then in 1971 the Court took its first turn toward the noose: in *McGautha v. California*, it held that a condemned person's constitutional rights were not violated "by permitting the jury to impose the death penalty without any governing standards" or by permitting the imposition of the death penalty in "the same proceeding and verdict as determine the issue of guilt." At that point, it looked like the string might have been played out; there were no more "narrow" procedural grounds. The Court would have to confront the ultimate issue. But it was not the same Court that had been sitting when the strategy was originally devised; there were four new Nixon appointees, and it was clear that at least some of them believed the death penalty to be constitutional. The umpires—if not the rules—had been changed after the strategy of the game had been worked out and irretrievably put into action. Now there was no pulling back.

The drama intensified. The Court let it be known that finally it was ready to decide the ultimate issue. Knowledgeable lawyers—counting noses on the Court—were predicting that the death penalty would be sustained. Some thought that it might be struck down for rape but sustained for murder. Some predicted that the Court would once again find—or contrive—a reason for avoiding the ultimate issue. A few, of optimistic bent, kept the faith and expressed the belief that the Court—even this Court—would simply not send hundreds to their death.

And then a major and unanticipated break. The California Supreme Court—perhaps the most influential state court in the nation—ruled that *its* constitution (which had substantially similar wording as the federal Constitution) forbade the death penalty. Then, on the last day of the United States Supreme Court's 1971 term, the decision was rendered: the death penalty, as administered in this country, was unconstitutional.

When the Court decided *Furman v. Georgia* in 1972, there were six hundred condemned prisoners awaiting execution on America's death rows. The Court ruled, in a 5–4 decision, that the death penalty, as implemented in the United States, was unconstitutional because of the randomness of its application. Never in the history of the courts had a single decision resulted in the saving of so many lives. Never in the history of the American judiciary had so many laws—both state and federal—been struck down with one judicial pronouncement. And never before had so important a social change been accomplished by the courts in so short a period of time.

In *Furman*, each of the five justices voting for reversal of the death sentence wrote separately, including Justice Brennan, who for the first time articulated his view that the imposition of the death penalty, under all circumstances, was per se unconstitutional. According to one commentator, Justice Brennan reached this conclusion using a mixture of "precedent, legal reasoning, moral imperatives, and over-all—hope—that the power of the Court could improve a society that appeared ambivalent about death as a punishment." Justice Brennan begins his attack on the death penalty in *Furman* by discussing the history surrounding the adoption of the Eighth Amendment and concluding that it is impossible to determine "exactly what the Framers thought 'cruel and unusual punishments' were." Given this ambiguity, Justice Brennan deemed it the Court's responsibility to interpret and apply this portion of the Eighth Amendment:

> The very purpose of a Bill of Rights was to withdraw certain sub-jects from the vicissitudes of political controversy, to place them beyond the reach of majorities and officials and to establish them as legal principles to be applied by the courts.

Were the Court to abdicate this responsibility, by blindly accept-ing the unreviewability of the power of the legislative branch to prescribe punishments for crimes, Justice Brennan warned that the "Cruel and Unusual Punishments Clause" would become, in short, 'little more than good advice.'"

Having decided that the courts must interpret the open-ended language of the clause, Justice Brennan reasoned that it "must draw its meaning from the evolving standards of decency that mark the progress of a maturing society." He then elaborated on this idea:

> At bottom, then the Cruel and Unusual Punishment Clause pro-hibits the infliction of uncivilized and inhuman punishments. The State, even as it punished, must treat its members with respect for their intrinsic worth as human beings. A punishment is "cruel and unusual," therefore, if it does not comport with human dignity.

In an effort to provide more specific content to the meaning of the phrase *does not comport with human dignity*, Justice Brennan offered the following test:

The test, then, will ordinarily be a cumulative one: If a punishment is unusually severe; if there is a strong probability that it is inflicted arbitrarily; if it is substantially rejected by contemporary society; and if there is no reason to believe that it serves any penal purpose more effectively than some less severe punishment, then the continued infliction of that punishment violates the command of the Clause that the State may not inflict inhuman and uncivilized punishments upon those convicted of crimes.

Justice Brennan proceeded to analyze the death penalty under this paradigm, after which he concluded:

In sum, the punishment of death is inconsistent with all four principles: Death is an unusually severe and degrading punishment; there is a strong probability that it is inflicted arbitrarily; its rejection by contemporary society is virtually total; and there is no reason to believe that it serves any penal purpose more effectively than the less severe punishment of imprisonment. The function of these principles is to enable a court to determine whether a punishment comports with human dignity. Death, quite simply, does not.

Justice Brennan declared that the death penalty is surely the most severe and degrading punishment that society can inflict upon an individual, as evidenced by the following facts: the existence of a national debate over the death penalty where there is no such debate over other forms of punishment; the death penalty has been continually restricted by the states, and many have abolished it; death is reserved for only the most heinous crimes; cases in which the death penalty is available are treated differently by lawyers, judges, and state legislatures; the death penalty is unique in its finality and enormity; and, finally, the death penalty, unlike all other punishments, ensures that the executed person has "lost the right to have rights."

On the issue of arbitrariness, Justice Brennan began his argument with the observation that the death penalty is actually imposed very infrequently in modern society, with the numbers decreasing in every year since 1930, even though the population of the United States and the number of capital crimes committed by its citizens have been growing steadily. Based upon the fact that in a country of over 200 million people, fewer than fifty people per year were being executed, Justice Brennan argued that we should draw a strong inference of arbitrariness in the application of the death penalty. In response to the argument that these statistics can be explained by the fact that only the most "extreme" cases receive the death penalty, Justice Brennan observed that there is no logical distinction based in fact that separates those individuals who are condemned to die from those who are sentenced to life imprisonment. Justice Brennan also observed that the Court's prior decision in *McGautha v. California*, which rejected a defendant's claim that due process had been violated since the jury that condemned him was permitted to make that decision wholly unguided by standards governing the choice, serves to undercut the argument that the criminal justice system can systemically and nonarbitrarily separate the most "extreme" cases from the others.

Justice Brennan then turned to the third principle, whether a punishment has been rejected by contemporary society, and concluded that the death penalty has been almost totally rejected, both in the United States and in other countries. As circumstantial evidence of this conclusion, Justice Brennan noted that our society has gradually moved toward less inhumane methods of execution, from firing squads and hanging to lethal gas and "more humane" electrocutions, as well as the fact that public executions, once thought to enhance deterrence, have been completely done away with. In addition, the class of crimes for which the death penalty is actually being imposed is constantly shrinking; at the time Justice Brennan wrote his dissenting opinion in *Furman*, nine states had abolished the death penalty altogether, many others had not employed the punishment in many years, and the highest court of one state, California, had already declared that punishment unconstitutional under that state's counterpart of the Eighth Amendment.

The final principle that Brennan used to disqualify the death penalty from the range of possible punishments authorized by the

Eighth Amendment was the notion that a punishment may not be excessive in view of the purposes for which it is inflicted. The primary argument that Justice Brennan was required to answer is that execution deters murder and certain other heinous crimes better than life imprisonment. Justice Brennan first denied that the death penalty provides specific deterrence any better than life imprisonment; techniques of isolation, as well as focusing on the effective administration of the state's parole laws, can eliminate or minimize the danger of future crimes while the individual is confined. With respect to claims of increased general deterrence, Justice Brennan denied the possibility that there exist a significant number of persons in society who would commit a capital crime knowing that the punishment is long-term, perhaps even life imprisonment, but who would not commit the crime knowing that the punishment is death. In addition, although Justice Brennan admitted that the statistical evidence available in 1972 was inconclusive with respect to the deterrent value of the death penalty as opposed to life imprisonment, he buttressed his argument by observing that to a person contemplating a murder or rape, the risk of being executed, taking into account the method under which the death penalty was currently administered, was remote and improbable, whereas the risk of long-term imprisonment was near and great. Given these incentives, Justice Brennan concluded that there is simply no reason to believe, or any hard, statistical evidence to support, the claim that the death penalty provides greater deterrence, either general or specific, than does life imprisonment.

Aside from deterrence, Justice Brennan also rejected the suggestion that the death penalty serves the retributive goal of punishment any better than life imprisonment. First of all, Justice Brennan denied that a sentence of death, since it is inflicted so rarely in the United States relative to the number of capital crimes committed, serves to prevent private enforcement of the laws, to inculcate a respect for the laws in our citizens, or to satisfy some sense of just deserts for these criminals better than life imprisonment; in fact, he took the position that executing so few people actually undermines each of these values that comprise the retributive goal of punishment. Justice Brennan summed up his position in the following passage:

> When this country was founded, memories of the Stuart horrors were fresh and severe corporal punishments were common. Death was not then a unique punishment. The practice of punishing criminals by death, moreover, was widespread and by and large acceptable to society. Indeed, without developed prison systems, there was frequently no workable alternative. Since that time, successive restrictions, imposed against the background of a continuing moral controversy, have drastically curtailed the use of this punishment. Today death is a uniquely and unusually severe punishment. When examined by the principles applicable under the Cruel and Unusual Punishment Clause, death stands condemned as fatally offensive to human dignity. The punishment of death is therefore "cruel and unusual," and the States may no longer inflict it as a punishment for crimes. Rather than kill an arbitrary handful of criminals each year, the States will confine them in prison. "The State thereby suffers nothing and loses no power. The purpose of punishment is fulfilled, crime is repressed by penalties of just, not tormenting, severity, its repetition is prevented, and hope is given for the reformation of the criminal.

The moratorium on the imposition of the death penalty that had been achieved in *Furman* turned out to be short-lived. In 1976, a majority in *Gregg v. Georgia* reinstated the death penalty for murder on the ground that adequate procedural safeguards had been adopted that made the imposition of the death penalty no longer violative of the Eighth Amendment. In a dissenting opinion coauthored by Justice Marshall, Justice Brennan attacked the majority's holding.

The fatal constitutional infirmity in the punishment of death, they observed, is that it treats "members of the human race as non-humans, as objects to be toyed with and discarded. [It is] thus inconsistent with the fundamental premise of the Clause that even the vilest criminal remains a human being possessed of common human dignity." As such it is a penalty that "subjects the individual to a fate forbidden by the principle of civilized treatment guaranteed by the Clause." Justice of this kind is obviously no less shocking than the crime itself, and the new "official" murder, far from offering redress for the offense committed against society, adds instead a second defilement to the first.

In the cases following *Gregg v. Georgia*, Justice Brennan continued to adhere to his position that the death penalty is per se unconstitutional, offering additional arguments and statistical evidence to support this claim. For example, in his dissenting opinion in *McCleskey v. Kemp* (1987), Justice Brennan refuted the Court's claim that Georgia and other states have enacted appropriate safeguards to ensure fair determinations in the special context of capital punishment by citing a study that suggests that taking into account some 230 nonracial factors that might legitimately influence a sentencer, the jury more likely than not would have spared McCleskey's life had his victim been Black, instead of white. In addition, Justice Brennan cited statistics indicating that in Georgia, race accounts for a six-percentage point difference in the rate at which capital punishment is imposed, 11 percent for white-victim cases and 5 percent for Black-victim cases, and thus, the rate of capital sentencing in a white-victim case is 120 percent greater than the rate in a Black-victim case. These statistics provide support for Justice Brennan's arguments about the probability of arbitrary imposition of the death penalty that he first promulgated in *Furman*; however, rather than confirming his claim that the death penalty is *arbitrarily* imposed—that is, not imposed in only "extreme" cases—these statistics indicate that the death penalty is being systematically imposed against the killers of white victims more than the killers of Blacks.

In the following passage from *McCleskey*, Justice Brennan used these statistics to draw an analogy about the imposition of the death penalty to the burden of proof:

> In determining the guilt of a defendant, a State must prove its case beyond a reasonable doubt. That is, we refuse to convict if the chance of error is simply less likely than not. Surely, we should

not be willing to take a person's life if the chance that his death sentence was irrationally imposed is more likely than not. In light of the gravity of the interest at stake, petitioner's statistics on their face are a powerful demonstration of the type of risk that our Eighth Amendment jurisprudence has consistently condemned.

In addition to the statistical evidence, Justice Brennan also noted that prosecutors in Georgia have limitless discretion in the decision to seek the death penalty and that Georgia provides no list of aggravating and mitigating factors, or any standard for balancing them against one another, in making the sentencing determination. Both of these facts, Justice Brennan asserted, raise the specter of arbitrary enforcement of the death penalty and suggest reasons why the statistical evidence should be regarded as valid. In the concluding paragraph of his dissent in *McCleskey*, Justice Brennan made the following haunting statement:

> It is tempting to pretend that minorities on death row share a fate in no way connected to our own, that our treatment of them sounds no echoes beyond the chambers in which they die. Such an illusion is ultimately corrosive, for the reverberations of injustice are not so easily confined. "The destinies of two races in this country are indissolubly linked together," and the way in which we choose those who will die reveals the depth of moral commitment among the living.

Only time will tell whether the views of Justices Brennan and Goldberg on the constitutionality of the death penalty will ultimately prevail, as have the views of other great dissenters of the past. They surely will continue to prick the conscience of a nation that today seems bent on increasing the number of executions. Whatever the outcome of this great debate, Justice Brennan, along with Justice Goldberg, should certainly be credited with having helped to save the lives of more Americans who had been condemned to die than any judge in our history.

* * *

The possibility of innocent defendants being sentenced to death has been a concern since biblical times. It has occurred throughout history, including in the United States. One such notorious case involved Leo Frankl in the second decade of the 20th century. I wrote the draft of a play describing an ethical dilemma faced by lawyers involved in the matter. I distributed the draft to students in my Legal Ethics course at Harvard Law School. It generated feisty argument (see Appendix B).

Chapter 6

The Right to End One's Own Life

"Right to life" is asserted by those who would criminalize assisted suicide and abortion. Some "right-to-lifers" who favor the death penalty talk about "the right of innocent life." I wrote about the right to choose death over life in the context of an intriguing case of assisted suicide for which my client, Dr. Peter Rosier, was charged in Florida.

It was comparable to "a serialized gang murder," according to the director of the International Anti-Euthanasia Task Team. Not to be outdone, conservative commentator and former White House aide Patrick Buchanan likened it to acts committed by the Nazis under Adolf Hitler (acts that Buchanan has trivialized and sometimes even denied).[1]

What horrible deed warranted these comparisons? Mass murder? A gangland hit? A terrorist attack? No. At issue was the assisted suicide of a forty-three-year-old woman who, dying of a fast-spreading and painful form of cancer, decided to pick the time and circumstances of her death rather than leave it to the vagaries of her illness. Her husband, an eminent physician, was accused of murdering her with the assistance of her father.

The story is the kind of nightmare every family fears. A routine medical checkup, a suspicious finding, further tests—and then the

---

1   See Alan Dershowitz, *Chutzpah* (Boston, Little Brown & Co., 1991).

dread news: cancer. Every possible treatment and therapy is tried, but the cancer has spread throughout her body, even to her brain. It is hopeless, and death will not be painless and dignified. It will involve convulsions, vomiting blood, and indescribable pain.

Most families confronting the inevitability of a painful death simply let nature take its inevitable course. But a growing number of victims of incurable diseases are deciding to take control over their own dying. Patricia Rosier was one such cancer victim, whose decision to end her life with her family's assistance was compared to serialized gang murder and Nazi atrocities.

Although the media characterized her death as a "mercy killing," it is more aptly described as a "mercy suicide," because *she* made the decision to end her life, not her family or doctors. We don't even have a technical term for this growing phenomenon—a term akin to the rather cumbersome *euthanasia*, which is defined as "the act . . . of painlessly putting to death persons suffering from incurable conditions or diseases." In the absence of a pronounceable Greek term—*heosthanasia* will never catch on—I will stick to *mercy suicide*.

A mercy suicide, when committed by an adult of sound mind, is generally not a crime. In some religions it may be a sin to play God by hastening death even by minutes or hours. Under some philosophies, it may be morally wrong to deny oneself a few extra days of painful life. But regardless of philosophy or religion, no civilized society today should regard a terminal patient who attempted suicide as a criminal.

Mercy killing—the taking of the life of another person who is suffering and usually no longer sentient—is qualitatively different from mercy suicide in the eyes of the law. Indeed, it is fair to say that the eyes of the law—in most jurisdictions—are blind to the very notion of mercy killing. The letter of the law simply does not recognize mercy as a defense to murder: it regards all deliberate killing as murder, whether done in the name of love or hate. Although in practice most prosecutors close their eyes to such cases, vindictive or opportunistic ones occasionally will try to make a test case out of a mercy killing that has come to their attention.

The line between mercy suicide and mercy killing is not always crystal clear. Sometimes it is simply a function of timing or happenstance. When what was originally intended as an unassisted mercy suicide cannot be completed without the help of others, it becomes, in the eyes of a prosecutor, a criminal mercy killing.

That is essentially the Rosiers' story. What began as a clear case of mercy suicide by Patricia Rosier ended up with the trial of her husband, Peter, for first-degree murder, conspiracy to murder, and attempted murder.

The basic facts were not in dispute, but the legal consequences of those facts gave rise to one of the most contentious and emotional cases in Florida legal history.

Peter and Patricia met when they were thirteen and married at twenty-one, during his first year of medical school in New York. Peter became a doctor specializing in pathology and was eventually chairman of the pathology department at the local hospital in Fort Myers, Florida.

The two had been married for more than twenty years when Patricia was diagnosed as having cancer. They were a handsome couple—she a beautiful blonde, he with rugged good looks and boundless energy. They drove his-and-hers Rolls Royces, traveled to South America to hunt butterflies, and played a mean game of tennis. They lived in an expensive home on well-manicured grounds in an exclusive neighborhood of Fort Myers. Their living room was decorated with what the local newspaper described as "semi-nude photographs of Pat taken by a professional photographer." They had two teenagers.

Like other couples living in the fast lane of a slow town, the Rosiers' lives were not without controversy. Their somewhat ostentatious lifestyle generated resentment and gossip among some neighbors and colleagues. When Peter once strayed from his otherwise faithful devotion to Patricia—he had a brief affair with a hospital secretary several years before Patricia's illness—there was talk of divorce. But Peter ended the liaison, and the couple lived happily—until that terrible spring day in 1985 when a chest X-ray, part of a routine medical checkup, disclosed a suspicious shadow on Patricia's lung. Three days later a biopsy was performed at her husband's hospital. He was the pathologist in charge, and as soon as he looked at the slide, he knew that it was lung cancer. He decided to give up his practice to devote himself to caring for his wife and children.

The couple tried everything—surgery, chemotherapy, radiation. Nothing worked. Within months, four brain tumors were discovered, and there were no more treatment options. Patricia's doctors told her that if she terminated all treatment, she would die within hours, days, or—at most—weeks.

The pain was beginning to be unbearable. The vomiting of blood and pus was persistent. But Patricia remained emotionally strong and socially rational. She even appeared on television to lend strength to other cancer patients undergoing debilitating therapies. She discussed her situation with friends and continued to be a loving mother and wife.

Then she made that fateful decision to pick the time and circumstances of her death, not wanting to leave it to the unpredictable clock of the cancer. When she told her husband of her decision, Peter said that he would end his life with her. They had lived their entire lives together and would face death together. When the children learned of this, they pleaded with their father not to take his life. Losing both mother and father would be too much for them. Peter relented. No one tried to talk Patricia out of her decision to commit suicide, for two reasons: first, she had made up her mind; second, it wasn't really suicide, since her act would only hasten her imminent and painful demise.

Patricia selected the day and time of her death and planned a formal farewell dinner for her family.

Among those in attendance at the dinner, in addition to her husband and children, were her stepfather and her two half-brothers. Patricia had been alienated from her stepfather for many years, but past tensions between the two were forgotten, at least for the moment.

There was wine, and there were toasts. Patricia wore an elegant dress and had had her nails polished. Despite her pain, she wanted to look beautiful for her last evening, wanting to leave her family with glowing memories. After dinner they watched a video of the movie *Harold and Maude*, about an elderly woman who commits suicide to prevent herself from "growing old." When it was over, Peter Rosier and his wife retired to the bedroom and made love, drank some more wine, and made love again. After bidding farewell to family members, Patricia Rosier took twenty pills that she had selected for her suicide. One relative recalled that she described them as "jellybeans," so anxious was she to end her suffering. She quickly fell into a coma. She expected never to awake—to drift into a quiet and dignified death.

But something went wrong. The coma began to lighten. She had obviously taken too few pills to induce death. Would she awaken or remain comatose? Would there be brain damage? Pain? Emotional turmoil? No one could know. All Peter knew was that his wife did not want to awaken. She had determined to die. What was his obligation to his comatose wife? Would he be breaking his final promise to her if he did not assist her in achieving her goal: a painless and dignified death? He could not ask her advice. The decision was his to make, but it was her decision—she had already made it and acted on it, albeit incompletely.

"I administered something to her to terminate her life," Peter Rosier recalls. That something was morphine, a painkiller that is lethal at sufficient dosage. But the morphine was insufficient, and Patricia continued to breathe. While Peter was outside the house, pacing and crying, Patricia's stepfather decided to end her life by suffocating her. He placed his hands over her nose and mouth. In his own words, "She was alive before I took my hands and put them over her face. She was dead when I removed my hands."

Peter didn't learn at the time what had happened inside the bedroom. Her stepfather and brothers simply informed him that Patricia was dead.

For about a year, the circumstances surrounding Patricia's death remained a family secret. Then Peter decided to write a book about his late wife's courage. After completing a first draft, Peter gave an interview to a local television reporter in which he related what he believed were the circumstances of his wife's death, still unaware that her stepfather had administered the coup de grâce.

As soon as that interview was aired, the local prosecutor began an investigation. As part of the information-gathering process, the authorities wanted to interview Patricia's stepfather. Through his lawyer, he demanded total immunity from prosecution for himself and his sons as a condition of being interviewed. That should have tipped off the authorities that he had something to hide. But instead of asking for a "proffer"—a truthful outline of the facts—before deciding whether to grant immunity, the prosecutor acceded.

With blanket immunity, the stepfather disclosed for the first time that he had actually caused Patricia's death by suffocation. The prosecutors were dumbfounded. They had committed a blunder feared by every law-enforcement official: they gave the wrong person immunity. But they could not back out of their deal. The only possible target now was Peter Rosier.

Despite the certainty that Peter had not actually killed his wife, and despite the certainty that she wanted to take her own life, the prosecutor treated the loving husband as if he were indeed the triggerman in a serialized gang murder. Peter Rosier was indicted on charges of first-degree murder and conspiracy to murder. The prosecution's theory was that the stepfather's ultimate act was merely the final stage in a family conspiracy of which Peter was the architect and main participant.

Suddenly Peter Rosier found himself in jail, facing a possible death sentence in a state that has one of the highest execution rates in the country. He called me from prison on the day of his arrest and asked me to help him. I worked with his local lawyer to get him out on bail and to formulate the legal strategy used in his trial. In the event of his conviction, I was to be his appellate lawyer.

It was a groundbreaking case. Whatever verdict the jury or court would reach in this case would *become* the precedent for cases of this kind.

The defense was relatively straightforward. This was a mercy suicide, not a mercy killing. It was the will of Mrs. Rosier, not that of Dr. Rosier, that led to her death. Neither did her husband wish her to die nor did he kill her. The cancer caused her death, in the sense that but for the terminal illness she would still be alive. She herself determined the time of her death. And the ultimate means of her death was selected and implemented by her stepfather without consultation with Dr. Rosier. If this was a mercy killing, it was carried out by Mrs. Rosier's stepfather, not her husband.

Notwithstanding this defense, the jury could probably have convicted Dr. Rosier of attempted murder on the basis of existing law. True, he did not initiate the dying process—that was done by Mrs. Rosier, who swallowed the pills by herself. True, he did not administer the coup de grâce—that was done by Mrs. Rosier's stepfather. But Dr. Rosier did acknowledge to a reporter, on videotape, that after his wife's initial coma began to lighten, he "administered something to her to terminate her life." This could be enough, under the strict letter of the law, to constitute an attempt to commit murder.

The jury had to be convinced, therefore, not to follow the strict letter of the law, but, rather, to rule in the spirit of the law—to serve as the conscience of the community. The jurors had to be made to wonder what they would have done under such excruciating circumstances. And they had to be made to conclude that criminal law should not sit in judgment over loving family members who had to make a tragic choice between keeping a promise to a comatose loved one or abandoning her in a moment of crisis.

The trial was punctuated by heated exchanges and emotional outbursts. Peter Rosier cried when the evidence of his wife's suffering was introduced. His local trial lawyer, Stanley Rosenblatt of Miami, did an excellent job persuading the jury that the murder statutes were put on the books not for loving husbands like Peter Rosier, but for brutal killers like Charles Manson and Ted Bundy. He tried the case with emotion and empathy, inviting the jurors to put themselves in the unenviable situation Peter faced on that terrible night. The prosecutor, on the defensive for having given Patricia's stepfather immunity before he knew the facts, played the avenging angel. He demanded that the jurors simply apply the law to the facts and not distinguish among murders on the basis of motive.

The jury understood—even if the prosecutors and others did not—the differences between love and hate, between a self-willed, voluntary death and an involuntary death imposed by others. After weeks of trial, it took the jury only a few hours to acquit Peter Rosier of all criminal liability. The prosecution had lost all credibility by asking the jury to treat Dr. Rosier as if he were the functional equivalent of a gangland killer. Had the prosecution charged Dr. Rosier with assisting the suicide of another—which is a crime under Florida law—it might have had a better shot at a conviction. But by *overcharging* him with first-degree murder, it made it difficult for the jury to take its case as anything but a misguided vendetta.

Although jury verdicts have no formal precedent-setting effect, highly publicized jury acquittals such as this one have an impact on other juries throughout the country. Jurors often remember what other jurors did in similar cases, and this may give them the courage to do likewise. More important, politically motivated prosecutors follow jury verdicts the way arbitrageurs follow takeover rumors. One highly publicized acquittal may constitute a trend to a prosecutor anxious to avoid the embarrassment of a highly visible loss. An acquittal of the kind delivered in the Rosier case thus becomes a kind of self-fulfilling prophecy: the strong chance of an acquittal frightens prosecutors away from pursuing comparable cases.

The impact of the Rosier acquittal probably transcended cases involving terminal cancer patients. There have been reports of AIDS patients being helped with their suicides.

Inevitably, there will be more prosecutions, despite the Rosier acquittal. And in some of these cases, there will probably be greater doubt about whether the dead person truly wanted to be put out of his or her misery. It is possible, as opponents of mercy killing have argued, for there to be abuses. Sometimes family members and doctors are more anxious for the loved one's demise than is the loved one.

The potential for abuse will become even more troubling in light of medical advances. As sick people live out "technological lives" in which bodily functions are maintained by machines while the quality of life is sapped, there will be more and more terminal patients seeking to control their own dying. As Dan Callahan, an ethicist at the Hastings Center, a bioethical think tank, recently put it, "It is an increasing terror of medical progress. . . . People feel the only way they can regain self-control is to have available the possibility of sui-cide." As long as these patients retain the mental capacity to choose and leave unambiguous evidence of that choice, as Patricia Rosier did, there should be few problems beyond the occasional vindictive prosecutor.

But where the patient is insufficiently rational to make the choice, the law will have to devise rules to assure that the decision to terminate life is made out of love, not out of convenience or other less noble motives.

As academics and ethicists publicly debate the theoretical pros and cons of legalizing mercy killing and mercy suicide, the reality is that a great many friends and relatives assist in suicides, and a great many doctors subtly practice euthanasia. It is impossible to know the extent of such acts, since they are accomplished around the privacy of the deathbed. But in preparing for the defense of the Rosier case, I learned that they are far more widespread than might be suspected.

The prevalence of this practice leads some academics to call for its legalization and regulation, while others see it as an argument in favor of more vigorous enforcement of existing laws prohibiting all mercy killing. Medical ethicist Arthur Caplan recently warned a standing-room-only audience of the American Public Health Association that giving doctors "a license to kill would seriously undermine the trust between patient and doctor." Sick people have enough to worry about without always having "in the back of their head" the fear that their doctor may be planning to end their suffer-ing without asking them. This fear was exacerbated when an anon-ymous doctor wrote in a prominent medical journal boasting of how he decided to pull the plug on a patient he regarded as terminal.

There is no immediate likelihood that we may see the enactment of new laws legalizing or regulating the dying process in circum-stances such as those the Rosiers faced. In the meantime, anyone who assists in a mercy suicide or participates in a mercy killing risks prosecution, conviction, and imprisonment. Peter Rosier's acquit-tal somewhat reduces those risks, but it does not eliminate them. The risks increase when there is no evidence that the dead person actively sought to end his or her life and are also probably more serious for doctors than for family members. And they also are surely greatest when the act is publicized, rather than handled discreetly.

The risks are lowest when there is taped or documentary evidence that it was the terminal patient's decision to end his or her life and that the decision was rational and unambiguous. A living will, executed well in advance of the actual decision, won't be nearly as helpful as a contemporaneous and unambiguous expression of intention.

Mercy killing and mercy suicide are so fraught with emotion that our legal systems will never be able to treat them in an entirely logical manner. They will continue to be practiced in the netherworld of dying without express legitimation by our legal system. There are inherent tensions between the need to assure that the precious gift of life is not taken too casually and the desirability of keeping government a decent distance from an individual's deathbed. In the Rosier case, the Florida prosecutors demonstrated that they could not distinguish between an act of love and an act of murder. Fortunately for Peter Rosier—and for others confronting similar tragedies—the jury understood that a loving husband who helps his pained wife die in dignity is not a criminal. But other juries could rule differently. An act of love that causes the death of another is still an act of civil disobedience in many jurisdictions fraught with the danger of prosecution. It takes courage to confront death. It takes courage to challenge the law. Peter Rosier and his late wife were courageous people.

CHAPTER 7

Do Dead People Have the Right to Keep Their Organs?

———

M any people have living wills, allowing their usable organs to be transplanted upon their death to those in need of them. In the absence of such a will, some families consent after the death of a relative. But too many human beings die needlessly, because they cannot receive lifesaving organs of people who have already died. I have written controversially about this death-life issue.

It would be a win-win situation if more people donated their organs to be transplanted after they die. But many people and their families refuse to do so. At this point in our history, human beings have a right, recognized by law, to be buried along with their organs, even when these organs could be used to save the lives of other human beings. There may come a time in the future when people who are dying of organ failure may claim a right to use the organs of dead people. How would a moral society evaluate this claimed right? Before we seek to answer this question, it will be useful to look more broadly at the role of social institutions in dealing with human nature, particularly as it relates to the death-life decisions regarding the human body.

Law, religion, custom, tradition, and morality all share in common certain mechanisms for influencing and improving human conduct—for making it less "natural." These mechanisms are premised on the assumption that in the absence of external rules of conduct, most humans would tend to act selfishly (I define *selfish* to include family). The rules are designed to discourage human beings from making individualized ad hoc decisions based on a selfish cost-benefit analysis of the particular situation confronting them. Instead, they impose on individuals the obligation to think more generally, more broadly, more categorically, more altruistically, and more communally—that is, more morally. These rules prohibit different categories of acts. Some prohibit core evils, such as the killing of innocent people. Others prohibit acts that are not in themselves immoral, but that are thought to lead to core evils. Such prohibited acts include driving too fast or while drunk. Yet other rules seem designed simply to condition people to accept limitations—even artificial limitations—on their appetites or instincts. These include ritual restrictions on the eating of certain foods or the performance of certain ritually impure acts.

The rules of law, religion, and morality seek to make it more difficult to act on the instinct of selfish preservation of individual and family and to make it acceptable—indeed, obligatory—to act on the basis of a broader principle. The specific principle may vary depending on whether one is a Kantian, a utilitarian (act or rule), a believer in the Bible, or a follower of any other set of rules, but the mechanism is similar: it requires you to act not as if yours were the only situation, but as if it were part of a principled set of mutually binding obligations.

Consider, for example, the issue of cannibalism. Start first with the eating of a human being who has already died. Absent the constraints of law, morality, religion, and so on, any rational starving person—say, a sailor in a lifeboat, a soldier lost in a jungle, an entire city besieged and surrounded—would not think twice about eating the fresh meat of a dead person, any more than he or she would think about eating the fresh meat of a dead animal. Some might argue that it is "natural" for human beings to be revolted by the thought of eating the flesh of fellow human beings, even if they were not responsible for their death. But throughout history and throughout the world, people have eaten dead humans. We are revolted by the thought because law, morality, and religion have conditioned us to become revolted. If we had grown up in a world in which the eating of human flesh was common, we would not be revolted by such a diet any more than by our diet of animal flesh. Perhaps someday when artificial food becomes an easy alternative, our great-grandchildren will be as disgusted by the prospect of eating the flesh of animals who were once alive as my grandparents and parents were revolted by the thought of eating certain dead animals such as pigs and lobsters.

Why, then, do we not eat human flesh? For some, the answer is simple: God has told us not to. But the gods of the Polynesians said it was permissible. What if our God had said it was permissible? Putting the same question at a different level of abstraction: why did our God—or those who have purported to speak in his name—single out the flesh of humans as prohibited food? It seems a waste in a world in which so many are starving. Perhaps the answer lies in the slippery slope. If we would permit the eating of the flesh of someone who was already dead, we might be more inclined to kill them for their food value, just as we do with animals. So, we create a prophylactic rule—or, to use the words of the Talmud, we build a fence around the core prohibition. The core prohibition is the killing of human beings; the fence is the prohibition against the eating of already-dead human beings.

Perhaps there is another core principle behind not allowing the eating of human flesh. Is it that somehow the human body is sacred? That it should never be used as a means toward the end of saving another human life? Surely the answer to those questions must be no, as evidenced by the fact that we do not prohibit the harvesting of body organs of dead human beings for transplantation into live human beings who might otherwise die for lack of a needed organ. In principle, what is the difference between "harvesting" the flesh of dead human beings to save the lives of other human beings and "harvesting" their other organs? It cannot be personal preference alone. If it were, I might personally reject the distinction, unless someone could make a persuasive argument in support. If I were dead, I would just as soon have my flesh eaten in order to save the life of another human being as have my heart or kidneys removed for transplant. I make no claim to ownership of my body once dead, as evidenced by the fact that I have signed on as an organ donor. If there were a place to sign on as a flesh donor, I would do that as well—unless a larger principle were at stake.

There is, of course, this difference between transplanting an organ and eating the flesh. The organ is generally needed to save life. There is a one-to-one correlation. Eating human flesh, on the other hand, could become an appetite rather than a necessity. Indeed, we accept the eating of human flesh when absolutely necessary to save life, as in shipwrecks and following the famous airplane crash in the Andes in 1972. We just don't want it to become routine. We might develop the same attitude toward organ transplants if people began to transplant the blue eyes of dead people for purely cosmetic reasons.

Even—perhaps especially—when organs are needed to save lives, we properly worry that transplantation may encourage the killing of some human beings for their organs. Such practices are believed to exist in certain parts of the world even today, and we have built fences to protect the living from being killed for their organs. No moral, religious, or law-abiding person would order an organ if he knew someone would be killed to provide it. If we chose, we could build an even higher fence: namely, prohibit the use of the organs of the dead, just as we prohibit the use of their flesh.

When organ transplantation first became possible, some religious groups made precisely that argument: the human body is sacred; it must be buried with all its organs; removal of any organ, even if necessary to save human life, is a desecration. That is no longer the position taken by mainstream religions, most of which now tolerate, or encourage, organ donation (some encourage only the receipt of organs, not their donation, but that is an unacceptably selfish moral position). Moral leaders should encourage their followers to think of their corpses as containing living recyclable parts. This change in perspective should be made in the interests of saving human life, thereby enhancing rather than diminishing its value. A dead body whose usable organs have been removed should become a symbol of respect for the living body. It is all a matter of how we view it and what we teach our children. There is nothing "natural" or "unnatural" about cutting up a dead body to give life to a live one, whether by using its heart or its flesh.

To encourage respect for the living, we mandate respect for the dead. It is not so much that a dead person has rights in his remains, as that the living have rights to see the bodies of their loved ones treated with respect. It is a crime to desecrate a cemetery or a corpse. We require our pathologists to perform autopsies in a dignified manner. We dispose of body parts with respect. Soldiers risk their lives to recover the bodies of their fallen comrades. We do all this not because it matters to the dead but because it matters to the living. We have learned the lessons of history, which teach that societies that disrespect the dead bodies and resting places of the deceased tend to devalue the living bodies—the lives—of their contemporaries. What constitutes respect—burying a body *with* its organs or *without* them—is a matter of education and nurture rather than divine law or nature. In some societies, respect for the dead requires that the body be taken to a remote hilltop so that its flesh may be consumed by birds of prey. The circle of life!

The same can be said about abortion. Some who argue against abortion say that if we trivialize the "death" of a living human fetus, it becomes easier to devalue the life of a baby, a mentally retarded person, a prisoner, a Jew, a Black, an enemy, a stranger. Others argue that to compel a woman to bring an unwanted baby into the world devalues the life of the child and the welfare of the mother. Again, there is no one naturally correct answer for all moral people.

Another, less compelling example of a fence around the core violation would be the prohibition against selling and trading ivory. There's nothing wrong, in principle, with using the tusks of dead elephants. But once a trade in ivory becomes acceptable, live elephants will be killed for their tusks. Accordingly, we try to make ivory an immoral and illegal commodity.[1] Likewise with those who

---

1   Ivory, unlike food or transplantable organs, is not a necessity. It is a luxury. But for those whose livelihoods depend on securing and selling this luxury, the line between luxury and necessity blurs.

would try to make the wearing of animal fur unacceptable. Again, we can distinguish in principle between stripping the fur from dead animals and killing animals for their fur, but the lesson of history is that permitting the former will encourage the latter. Thus, we see the same principle in operation once again: we impose a seemingly irrational prohibition against a harmless use of resources—the flesh of dead people, the tusks of dead elephants, the fur of dead animals—in order to discourage a violation of the core principle, namely, killing to secure these same commodities.

There are, of course, intermediate approaches. We could impose harsh punishments on those who kill elephants for their tusks while encouraging the use of tusks from elephants that died naturally. Experience would then show whether it is necessary to have a blanket prohibition on the sale (or use) of all tusks in order to prevent the killing of elephants. Or we could distinguish between the use of fur from animals specifically bred and raised for their fur and from animals in the wild. In the end, it will be experience rather than some abstract natural rule that will determine how high we need to build the fence in order to protect the core value.

The very concept of a fence is a recognition that rights are built on our experience with wrongs. It is this experience that cautions us about the dangers of the slippery slope—about the inclination of some people to take arguments to the limits of their logic and beyond. The great irony is that it is experience with moral relativism, situational ethics, and continua that leads some to argue for absolutes and clear lines, and to pretend (or persuade themselves to believe) that these absolutes and lines come from God or nature.

The argument for absolutes and clear lines, rather than for continua, is a plausible one, based on human experience. It is played out regularly in our courts, as some judges read provisions of our Constitution as absolute prohibitions on governmental power, while others read exceptions and a rule of reason into these same provisions. Justice Hugo Black argued that the First Amendment's statement that Congress "shall make no law . . . abridging the freedom of speech" meant what it said: no law means *no exceptions*. Justice Felix Frankfurter argued for a rule of reason pursuant to which the government could make laws abridging certain genres of dangerous or offensive speech. When a government lawyer would argue for an exception, Black would take out his worn copy of the Constitution and read, "Congress shall make no law. . . ," banging the table as he shouted the word *no*. Frankfurter would then mock Black by opening his copy of the Constitution and reading the same words, except that he would bang the table when he shouted the word *Congress*, emphasizing the fact that the literal prohibition applies only to one branch of the federal government, not to the states or to the executive or judicial branches.

Black was a legal positivist and a pragmatist. He did not believe that the absolutes he insisted on came from God or nature. Instead, he thought the Framers had decided to impose absolute prohibitions on certain governmental actions as a result of their negative experiences with judicial discretion and slippery slopes. Frankfurter placed greater trust in elite judges and in their ability to interpret constitutional prohibitions in a reasonable manner. Both were products of their own very different experiences, Black as a populist legislator, Frankfurter as an elitist professor.

The debate over whether absolute prohibitions or relative continua provide better protection against slippery slopes should be an empirical one that can be resolved by human experiences rather than by the Delphic voices of God or Nature.

Let us now try to apply the experimental approach to a specific set of questions relating to organ donation A friend of mine recently died because he was unable to get a suitable heart for transplant. No healthy hearts were available at the time he needed his transplant, and so in order to remain alive he had to settle for the heart of a patient with hepatitis. The heart transplant worked, but my friend soon died of liver failure.

My friend, unfortunately, is among the large number of Americans who needlessly die each year because other Americans selfishly refuse to donate lifesaving organs after their own deaths. In the United States, there is a presumption against organ donation at death, which can be overcome only if the potential donor has made an affirmative decision to consent to having his or her organs removed upon death. In many European countries, the presumption goes the other way: all people are presumed to consent to the lifesaving use of their organs unless they explicitly take action to withhold consent. The result is that many more organs are available for transplant patients in European countries than in our own.

I can imagine few more selfish and immoral acts than insisting that your lifesaving organs must be buried with you so that worms can eat them, rather than allowing them to be used by other human beings to save their lives or to restore sight. Yet many Americans refuse to consent to organ donation upon death. A significant number justify their act of selfishness by reference to their religion. But what kind of religion would preach that it is wrong to help save lives by donating organs from a dead body? Religious leaders should be in the forefront, urging their followers to overcome their fears and superstitions and take the simple step that will directly save lives.

But religious leadership alone will not eliminate the critical shortage of organs. We need to change the law. At the very least, we should move toward the European system of presuming consent in the absence of explicit withholding of consent Even this shift of presumption may not produce enough organs. The time has come to raise the question of who owns a person's life-giving organs after that person has died. Do you have a right to have buried or cremated parts of your body that could keep other people alive? Would it violate the rights of dead people or their families for a state to pass a statute mandating organ removal and reuse after death? (There already are statutes requiring the removal and preservation of organs when autopsy is mandated for evidentiary purposes.) Would there have to be an exception for religious objection? There are questions we ought to begin debating. Improvements in medical technology require us to rethink old attitudes about our bodies after death. Treating the dead body with respect is an important element of humanity, but the forms of respect may vary. We as a society might well—and should—come to believe that retrieving organs that can then be kept alive and given to others is a proper way of showing respect.

When organ transplants first became feasible, many traditionalists objected—on moral and religious grounds—to playing God and tinkering with nature. Over time, attitudes changed, and almost nobody today *turns down* a lifesaving organ on religious or moral grounds. The Golden Rule—which is central to Judaism, Christianity, Islam, and other religions—requires that we treat our neighbors as ourselves. Anyone willing to *accept* a transplant must be willing to give their own organs. Religions that permit their adherents to receive transplants *must* permit them to donate organs, lest they be accused of hypocritically violating the Golden Rule. Perhaps an additional encouragement to transplant donation would be a rule excluding all adults who had not consented to donating their organs from receiving the organs of others. At least there should be a preference for those who were willing to donate organs.

Anyone who refuses to sign the box on the driver's license application, which constitutes consent to removal of organs after death, is either a coward, a fool, a knave, or a slave to superstition or religious fundamentalism. There is no softer way of putting this. It is simply wrong to waste the organs of the dead when they can be used to give life. It is understandable that some relatives of a crash or shooting victim would not be willing to consent to the removal of organs from the bodies of their recently deceased loved ones. But it is not understandable for an adult to refuse to consent in advance to the life-giving use of his own otherwise useless organs. We should make such selfishness unacceptable as a matter of morality and perhaps even as a matter of law.

Eventually our experiences with organ transplantation may move our society toward the recognition that there should be no right to refuse to have your organs harvested for lifesaving use after your death. There should, of course, be a right not to have your death accelerated in order to maximize the chances that your organs can most effectively be used. That should be a matter of choice. And there should, of course, be a right not to be killed in order to have your organs used to save the life of a more important or wealthier person. We might need fences around these core principles, but there is the danger that a fence built too high may endanger other core values.

Organ transplantation provides a good example of important values clashing with others. First there is the claimed value in preserving intact the bodily integrity of a dead loved one, or even the right of the dead person to dispose of his body as he chooses. On the other side of the ledger is the value of preserving the life of the person in need of an organ. Does a live person have the right to the organ of a dead stranger if that organ, and that organ alone, means the difference between life and death? What if the person in need of the organ is a scientist on the verge of curing cancer, the president of the United States, or a single mother of two children? Does their right to live—and our right to have them live—outweigh the right of the deceased to be buried with all his organs? Will it really make a difference if he is buried with one less kidney, no liver, or no heart?

Of course, much depends on how the issue is framed. Instead of describing the choice as between the life of the recipient and the wish of a dead person, it could be described as between the right of a human being to make important decisions about the disposition of his body and the power of the state to compel that person to violate his religious, moral, or aesthetic principles. Thus, the framing of rights issues exerts a powerful influence on the moral and political debate and can be used to tilt the debate toward a favored position. Some religious and political leaders are particularly adept at this, and advocates on all sides of contentious issues employ these framing tactics.

In general, our society gives individuals considerable authority to direct the disposition of their property after their death, but this right is not without some limits. A husband may not completely disinherit his wife. Nor may he deny the government its statutory share of his property—namely, the inheritance tax. A body is, of course, different from a bank account or even a valuable painting. Even with regard to a painting, however, there may be some limits. If a private person who owned an important collection of early Picasso paintings maliciously decided to have them destroyed upon his death, some societies—France, for example—would prohibit such a destruction of what is deemed a national treasure.[2] In the United States, some

---

2 Franz Kafka's literary executor refused to follow Kafka's instructions to burn his unpublished manuscripts and instead had them published.

privately owned buildings are declared historical landmarks and may not be destroyed, even if destruction is in the private financial interests of the owner. All governments assert the power of eminent domain over property needed for certain public purposes.

There may come a time when our collective experience with organ transplantation causes us to disregard (or give less weight to) the wishes of dead persons and their families if their organs could save lives. If experience shows that widespread organ retrieval saves numerous lives at little cost—psychic, moral, and financial—a consensus may emerge regarding lifesaving organs as "rightfully" belonging to those most in need of them. If that were to occur, many more people would probably begin to donate their organs, and there would be less need for mandatory confiscation. But if there were still a shortage, a mandatory system might be considered.

Experience could, on the other hand, move us in the opposite direction. It could turn out that more frequent organ transplantation produces negative consequences, such as hastening the deaths of sick people with needed organs, diminishing the value we place on the human body, discouraging research on other lifesaving techniques, or creating a caste system in which certain recipients are preferred over others. If that were to be our experience, then it might well reinforce current attitudes against having one's body "cut up" after death. The point is that there is no natural or divinely mandated way of showing respect for the human body. Deciding whether to regard the dead human body as an integral entity to be buried intact, rather than as an expired container for recyclable lifesaving organs, is very much a matter of experience. As experiences change, so do attitudes and so do rights—even rights as emotionally laden as the claimed right to be buried or cremated with one's organs intact.

One final word about consistency of principle. Opponents of abortion emphasize the right to life, or potential life, but many of them oppose organ donation, especially if it is mandatory. Living people remaining alive is more important than dead people being buried with their potentially lifesaving organs being available for maggots to eat. So, to be consistent, right to life antiabortion advocates should be on the forefront of the campaign for organ donation.

CHAPTER 8

The Holocaust

The worst example of human-caused death on a large scale was the Holocaust, in which six million Jews were systematically murdered as part of Hitler's genocidal "final solution" to what he described as "The Jewish Problem"—which meant the very existence of the Jewish people. Following the defeat of the Axis in 1945, the leaders of Nazi Germany and Fascist Japan were placed on trial Some were convicted, others acquitted. Many, including hands-on mass murderers were never brought to trial, or were pardoned, or their sentences commuted, after conviction. The result was that the slogan "Never Again" became the reality of "Again, again, and again," as genocides and genocide-like mass killings were repeated in Cambodia, Darfur, and other parts of the world in the decades following the Holocaust.

I have been obsessed with the horrors of the Holocaust and the world's inadequate response to it for most of my life. I wrote a novel, *Just Revenge*, about one person's efforts to achieve justice. And I am now working on an opera libretto based on one person's death-and-life decision during the Holocaust. I present it here as a work in progress.

Libretto for *Hinnini*[1]

The first scene of the first act takes place in the great synagogue of Warsaw on Rosh Hashana of 1940. A male choir hums the wordless melody that traditionally begins the high holiday services. The cantor, Gershon Sirota—a striking man with a black beard, wearing a white high hat and tallit—ascends the bimah and turns to the open Torah Arc. He begins his soliloquy in Hebrew to the traditional tune: "*Hinnini He'ani Mi'maas, Nirash V'nifchad M'pachad Yosheve T'hilot Yisrael.*"

The choir translated to English:

"Here I stand impoverished in deeds. Trembling before the Lord."

The cantor continues: "*Bati Laamod Ul' his chanein Lfraecha Al amcha Yisrael Asher Shlachuni.*" The choir translates, "I have come before you on behalf of your people Israel who have sent me although I am personally unworthy to do so."

The cantor then whispers the words "*V*"*na Al Tafsheim B'Chatoise . . . Ki Chotsy Ufoshea Ani.*" The choir translates: "Please do not hold them to blame for my sins and do not find them guilty for my inequities. For I am a sinner."

The cantor then raises his voice: "*V'kabel tfilasi ksvilas zakkain v'ragel, ufirko nae.*" The choir translates: "Accept my humble prayer as that of an elder whose beard is fully grown, whose voice is sweet."

Then, turning his head from the Torah Arc, the cantor looks directly at the German military guard who is standing near the exit and sings the Hebrew words: "*V'sigar B'satan L'val Yashtinaini.*" The actual translation of the Hebrew, understood by all in the audience, is: "May you denounce the Satan that he not impede me." When the choir translates, however, it repeats the Hebrew word *saton*, without translating it.

The cantor concludes the prayer in Hebrew: "*V'al yuhi shum machshol B'svilasi.*" The choir translates: "And may there be no stumbling block to my prayer."

---

1   This libretto is based on a real story of a great cantor who recorded with Caruso and was known as "The Caruso of the Synagogue."

The president of the synagogue, wearing a high black hat and tuxedo, ascends the bimah, faces the audience, and addresses them directly, in Yiddish, in a recitative to the tune of the original melody without words; the choir translates: "Jewish law requires obedience to the government in power.

In years past, we recited a prayer for the Polish government.

We are loyal Poles. We love our country. And we love the Jewish people.

The law of the land is our law, and we must comply with it whether we agree or not. Today the government of Poland is under the control of the German army. We need not pray for the success of these occupiers, but we must comply with their laws.

I have been chosen as a representative of the Jewish people in their dealings with the German occupiers.

I am the head of the *Judenrat*—the Counsel of Jews.

Cantor Sirota has been chosen as the representative of the Jewish people to God. We each must do our duty.

In my capacity as head of the *Judenrat* of Warsaw, I have been asked to take an oath of allegiance to the German occupiers.

I take this oath today on Rosh Hashana, knowing that in ten days we will recite the *Kol Nidre* prayer. I think you understand. Others among you will be required to take oaths, just as the Jews of the Inquisition were. '*Ushavuotana lo shavuot.*'" The choir does not translate these words, which mean that oaths made under such compulsion are not oaths!

"In the days leading up to Rosh Hashana, an area has been set aside in Warsaw exclusively for its many Jewish residents. A wall is being built and will soon be completed.

All Jews who live within the Warsaw ghetto will be required to remain here. All Jews who reside anywhere else in Warsaw will be obliged to move here.

This will require all of you to take in friends, neighbors, and strangers, as the Torah commands. Remember that you, too, have been strangers.

I am assured by the German commandant that if we comply with these orders, we will be allowed to live in peace.

Schools will remain open for all the children. The synagogues will continue to function. Cultural events will be allowed.

Some strong and healthy men and women will be transported to work camps where they will be required to help the German war effort.

Food will be in short supply, but I am assured it will be adequate to maintain health. Please cooperate with those in power. We have no choice.

Resistance would be futile and would cause recriminations against those of us who wish to live in peace with the occupiers.

The Jewish people have survived domination, repression, pogroms, and Ghettos. We will endure this oppression as well, as long as we comply with the rules. *Am Yisrael Chai.* The Jewish people live. '*Shana tova*, best wishes for a good New Year.'"

The choir then sings a verse from *Avinu Malkenu*, emphasizing and repeating the words "Our Father, Our King bless us with a good New Year."

Act 1, Scene 2

Scene 2 takes place in the home of Cantor Sirota on the eve of Yom Kippur. Sirota, his wife, and children, along with a dozen relatives and friends who have moved into the in-home pursuant to the German order, are eating the meal before the fast begins at sundown. They all join in the singing of *zemirot*—religious songs traditionally sung during festive meals.

Sirota stands up, pulls out a letter, and sings in Yiddish recitative. The female choir translates into English:

"I hold in my hand an invitation to perform Puccini's *Tosca* and Donizetti's *La Fille du Régiment* at the Metropolitan Opera in New York." He then sings the last few bars from "*E lucevan le stelle.*" "They picked me for my ability to sustain high Cs, which few tenors can do.

As you know, I have been in the United States before. It is a wonderful country. I love singing to Americans. And they love me. They play my recordings, along with Enrico Caruso's. They will welcome me with open arms.

The United States, which is not at war with Germany, has granted me a visa for six months.

But it is for me alone. Not my family or friends.

I must decide whether to accept.

The *Judenrat* has urged me to go and tell the Americans about our situation here in Warsaw. Perhaps President Roosevelt can help.

I am undecided. I fear that if I go, I will never be allowed to return, and my family and friends will remain unprotected. If I stay, my status as the chief cantor of Warsaw may accord them some protection.

What shall I do?

Shall I say *Hinnini* to the Americans who have made this generous offer? Or should I say *Hinnini* to my community and family?

What shall I do?"

Professor Avraham Ringel, Sirota's cousin, responds in his deep baritone voice:

"You must go and tell the world why they have gathered us into this walled Ghetto.

We are like sheep awaiting slaughter.

They will not kill us as long as the Americans do not enter the war.

They are desperate to keep Roosevelt neutral, despite Churchill's demands.

You must explain and urge the Americans to use their leverage to allow us to go to Palestine, where we will be safe. And the Germans and Poles will be rid of us, as they wish to be."

Another cousin, Dr. Mordechai Cohen, disagrees in his basso voice:

"They don't want to kill us. They need us to work. There are nearly a million of us. Many children. They can't kill us all.

Gershon, you must stay and encourage your community to comply with the orders of the *Judenrat*.

They respect you. They will listen to you instead of the Communists and radicals who call for resistance.

You can help save us. But only if you stay. There will be other opportunities to sing at the opera. Your duty is to us. You must sing God's prayers, not Verdi's arias. You must respond to our call by saying *Hinnini*—here I stand. In Warsaw. With us."

With tears in her eyes, Cantor Sirota's wife, in her soprano voice, pleads with her husband to save his own life: "You must go. Seek safety in America.

You are the messenger of our community to God. And to the World. They love you. They love your voice. They will listen to you.

They will listen to our voice only through your voice. It's power and beauty will persuade them as nothing else can. *Shma Koleinu.* Go. You will protect us from afar better than you can from here. Be our Moses and Aaron. It would be selfish for us to ask you to stay, because we love you. It will be selfless for you to go—alone, out of one wilderness into another. Only you can save us. Your *Hinnini* must be in America not in Warsaw. *Lech L'chca.* Go with God. It is *bashert*—your destiny."

Cantor Sirota relates a Chasidic story:

"A great rabbi and his best student were presiding over a marital dispute. After the wife told her side, the rabbi said: 'You are right, my daughter.'

Then the husband told his side. The rabbi responded: 'You are right, my son.'

The student said: 'But Rabbi, they can't both be right.' To which the rabbi responded: 'You, too, are right.'

Cousins Ringel and Cohen, you are both right. My dear and loving wife, you are right, as you always are.

Now I must choose between the right and the right. I will seek God's guidance." He then sings a variation on the traditional *Hinnini* prayer:

"Here I stand
Confused and uncertain.
Trembling before you Lord
I have been endowed with a beautiful voice
But not with a mind that matches it.
I am an ordinary man—a Ben Ani—with an extraordinary voice.
But the beauty of my voice hides my mediocrity as a person, a thinker, a decider.
You must decide for me. I will do your bidding.

Send me a sign. A message. A hint. Bring me peace. Help me choose between the right and the right. Save me from doing the wrong.

Here I stand. *Hinnini.*

On the eve of Yom Kippur. Bereft, lonely and frightened.

In an hour I will intone the following sacred words: '*Mi yom kipporim Zeh ad yom kipporim haba Aleinu l'tova.*' 'From this Yom Kippur until the next Yom Kippur that will come in goodness upon us.'

Yet none of us mere mortals even know whether we will live to see the next Yom Kippur.

We need your help. I need your guidance. *Caper lanu*—forgive us for we have sinned. Hoshana. Save us for we are your people. As I chant the ancient melody of the *Kol Nidre* legal formula, rescinding all vows, I will be looking and listening for a sign—a *simun*—from the Yeshiva *shel mala* to the Yeshiva *shel mata*. From the assemblage on high to the assemblage here on Earth. *Hinnini.* I stand in awe and await your guidance. For you do not rescind your vows to the Jewish people. *Avinu malkeinu shma koleinu.* Hear our prayers."

The company slowly leaves in the direction of the synagogue.

Act 2, Scene 1

The synagogue on Yom Kippur eve. The ark is open, and all the Torahs are being held by the rabbis and officers, as the Cantor intones the *Kol Nidre*. The orchestra is silent. The male choir translates: All vows, prohibitions, oaths, are rendered null and void. From this Yom Kippur to the next Yom Kippur, may it come upon us for good.

The cantor chants the *Kol Nidre* flawlessly and with passion—until he reaches the high c of the final sentence—Shavuot (vows). Then for the first time in his long career, he is unable to hit the high note. His voice cracks. Thinking that is simply a temporary problem, he repeats the word. Again, his voice cracks. The congregants who have heard him hit these notes effortlessly over the years and even as recently as Rosh Hashanah, are aghast. Again, he tries and again he fails. In frustration, he moves on to the rest of the service which he completes beautifully, because he is not required to reach any high notes. A cantor has the ability to adapt the liturgy to his personal vocal limitations.

Act 2, Scene 2

In the cantor's room behind the *bima*, his wife consoles him.

"The service was beautiful. One note doesn't change anything."

"But why? I've never had such a problem."

"Did you have your raw egg before service?"

"Yes. And my honey. It was something else. Something different."

"Could it be a sign? The sign you prayed for."

"What kind of sign would a failed high note be?"

Suddenly it occurs to the cantor. He pauses. Looks up to heaven and sings the last verses from the famous aria from *Tosca*, "*E lucevan le stelle*." When he comes to the high note, his voice cracks. He cannot reach it. He tries again. He fails.

"It is the sign."

"In what way?" his wife asks.

"Don't you see? I don't need to reach the high note to be a cantor. There are baritones, even basses. I can come down an octave at the end of *Kol Nidre*. But for Tosca, for *La Fille du Régiment*—for any opera—the tenor <u>must</u> be able to hit high C. He cannot vary a single note from what the composer wrote. I cannot go to America and sing opera. I would be a failure. A disgrace, a *shanda*. I must stay in Warsaw and sing *Hinnini, Kol Nidre, and avinu malkainu* with my broken voice. The sign is clear. Thank you, God, for sending it. And thank you for using my voice as the messenger, as the *shaliach tzibur*. How fitting. How *bashert*.

Now I know what I must do.

I must stay

I will stay.

Hinnini. Here I stand with my people."

Act 3, Scene 1

Act 3 is set in the spring of 1943, at the cantor's Passover Seder. The same people are there, except for Dr. Cohen and a sixteen-year-old boy named Elon. Everyone is suffering, emaciated, and bedraggled. The ghetto has taken its toll. The Seder plate is partially empty. They could get no greens or bitter herbs in the ghetto. A young boy alto chants the four questions. The cantor explains that although the bitter herbs are an essential part of the Seder, they are unnecessary in Warsaw in 1943.

"The bitter herbs—the *Morer*—are a symbol of the Jewish suffering in Egypt. In Warsaw, we don't require symbols of suffering. Here we have <u>real</u> suffering."

Mrs. Cohen cries as she recalls her husband's murder at the hands of Nazis. "For treating one of his Catholic patients, they shot him. They shot others, as well. Even children, for trying to escape.

Now there are rumors that they are closing the ghetto and sending all the residents to work camps—they call them concentration camps. Some call them death camps. We know the cities: Auschwitz, Treblinka, Bergen-Belsen, Sobibor.

There are also rumors of resistance. Even uprisings. The Communists, the young socialists and radical Zionists are organizing under a young man named Mordechai Anielewicz. A firebrand. Elon has joined them. He escaped through a sewer and is in the forest."

Mrs. Sirota worries: "They will make trouble for all of us. We should follow the *Judenrat*, who know what's best for the community."

Professor Ringel responds: "Can there be more trouble than we already have? God bless the resisters. I wish I were young enough to join them."

As the Seder continues, we hear noises outside. The resistance has begun. Jewish snipers are shooting at Nazi soldiers and throwing homemade bombs at the Nazi tanks that have entered the ghetto. The chazan sings the "*El Maleh Rachamim*"—the prayer for the dead—over the din of battle. Screams of death are all around.

Nazis break into the Sirota house. The cantor stands up and says, "*Hinnini*," I am here.

The Nazi leader says, "We have come for the singer. General Shoup wants him to remain in Warsaw to entertain the troops by singing opera. Only him. The rest must be deported to the camps."

Sirota sings his last aria—a variation on the *Hinnini* prayer:

"Here I stand

Together with my family

Ready to die in the name of the Almighty—*al kiddush Hashem.*

I will not plead for mercy at the hands of these murderers.

I will not sing for them—only for you God and your people, my people.

Satan had prevailed—for now. There is no hope for us.

My prayer now is for *nekama*—just revenge.

I am no longer unworthy and unqualified to have my voice reach the heavens. I stand bravely in the valley of the shadow of death. *Hinnini.*"

The opera ends with ferocious sounds of battle as the Sirota family is led to their inevitable deaths to the melody of *El Maleh Rachamin.*

* * *

Is Zelenskyy a Ukraine Holocaust Denier?

Volodymyr Zelenskyy has performed a truly great service on behalf of the Ukrainian people. Because of his Churchill-like determination to resist Russian aggression, I plan to propose him for the Nobel Peace Prize. But he has in the recent past mendaciously denied the role of Ukrainian people in the Holocaust. He has used that argument to demand that Israel owes Ukraine offensive weapons. He expressed shock that Israel hasn't capitulated to his demands, based on gratitude to Ukrainians for saving Jews during the Holocaust. He has never apologized for the following mendacious statement he made: "The Ukrainians made a choice eighty years ago, we saved Jews…"

He is right the Ukrainian people made a choice eighty years ago, but the choice was to <u>murder</u> Jews, <u>not save</u> them. The vast majority of Ukrainians were complicit with or supported the Germans in rounding up Jews and killing them in places like Babi Yar. Most certainly they didn't save Jews.

The complicity of Ukrainians in these mass murders was greater than in most other countries.

Thousands of Ukrainian Jews were murdered. Nor was this the first time that the Ukrainian people made a choice. In 1648, Bogdan Chmielnicki led a pogrom of women and children that resulted in the deaths of tens of thousands of Jews, including babies, children, and mothers. That was a long time ago, but the statue of this genocidal murderer still stands in the center of Kyiv, and his picture still adorns the Ukrainian five-dollar bill. That is now! Ukraine has made a choice: to honor the memory of a mass murderer of Jews.

Between the Chmielnicki murders and the Holocaust, the Ukrainian people made many other choices: they conducted pogrom after pogrom against Jewish families. Anti-Semitism was rampant throughout Ukraine. That is why so many Ukrainian Jews immigrated to the United States and elsewhere.

In recent years, the situation in Ukraine has improved measurably. Though there still is a large number of anti-Semites, including in certain units of the armed forces, the remembrance of the Holocaust has caused many Ukrainians to abandon the traditional anti-Semitism that plagued the country. They even voted for Zelenskyy, who is a man of Jewish heritage.

If Zelenskyy had made a nuanced statement acknowledging that the choice made by most Ukrainian people eighty years ago was to kill Jews and not save them, but that the situation is now improved, I would congratulate him for his honesty. But he knows—after all, he is himself of Jewish heritage—that the choice made by the Ukrainian people eighty years ago deserves to be condemned, not praised.

It has been said that the truth is the first casualty of war, but that is no excuse for perpetrating a lie that has now spread throughout Eastern Europe: namely, that Ukrainians, Poles, Latvians, Lithuanians, Estonians, Romanians, and Hungarians saved Jews. It is true that in each of these countries, there were brave men and women who risked their lives in an effort—mostly unsuccessful—to save Jews. The recent film by Ken Burns about the American role in the Holocaust singled out a Polish Catholic man who I knew named John Karski, who risked his life to go into death camps and report to the world what he saw. Others took similar heroic action. Many of them have been memorialized in Holocaust Museums as among the righteous. But the righteous were an infinitesimal percentage among the unrighteous in these countries. Ukraine may have been the worst of all. It was certainly not among the best.

In light of the actual history, Zelenskyy's ill-advised lie may well qualify as a variation on Holocaust denial or Holocaust minimization. By denying Ukrainian complicity in the mass murder of thousands of Ukrainian Jews, he has distorted history and memory.

I hope he understands that even desperate times—and he is certainly presiding over a country during desperate times—do not justify erasing the memory of the Ukrainian Jews who died at the hands of other Ukrainians. Zelenskyy is a great man, but great men often have great flaws. He has an opportunity to remedy his deep insult to the memory of the Jews who were killed as a result of immoral choices made eighty years ago by Ukrainians.

It may be true that some Ukrainians were forced or frightened into becoming complicit with the Nazis, but many more eagerly joined them, precisely because they wanted to murder Jews, not because they had to. History and truth have their claims, and yesterday's horrors must not be erased in the name of preventing today's.

I hope that Zelenskyy will become a Nobel Peace Laureate. It is essential, therefore, for him to correct and acknowledge that the choice made by "the Ukrainians" was a horrible and indefensible one.

Armenian Genocide Deniers and Holocaust Deniers

It is a historical fact that beginning in approximately 1915, the Ottoman Empire murdered hundreds of thousands of innocent Armenians. This was part of a program of ethnic cleansing and a desire by Turkish Muslim leaders to get rid of Armenian Christians. There is some dispute as to the precise number of Armenians killed, ranging from approximately 600,000 to double that number. There is also some dispute about the causes of this atrocity, especially the role of World War I. But no honest person can dispute the basic facts: namely, a decision was made by Ottoman authorities to exterminate and/or expel Armenians, and that the order was carried out largely by the military.

Why then do some people—even some decent people—refuse to recognize this historical event? Turkish authorities have done everything in their power to pressure individuals and countries not to acknowledge this genocide. They have done so by threats, extortion, and bribery. For many years these tactics worked. Indeed, it is reported that Hitler, in 1939, used the Armenian genocide as a way of assuring the German people that the world will not react to his planned genocide against the Jews. According to reports by eyewitnesses, he said the following to the audience: "Who remembers now the extermination of the Armenians?" Whether or not this is an exact quote, it accurately summarizes the lesson Hitler drew from the Turkish genocide against the Armenians: no one will really care if the Nazis exterminate the Jews.

Ken Burns's recent documentary on the Holocaust suggests that Hitler was probably right. Between 1939 and 1945, six million Jews—babies, children, women, the elderly—were murdered by gas chambers, shooting squads, and pogroms organized by local Ukrainians, Poles, Hungarians, Latvians, Lithuanians, Estonians, and others. Although after it was over, memorials have been built to commemorate this unspeakable tragedy, while it was occurring, most countries in the world—including the United States, Canada, and Great Britain—did worse than nothing: they willfully and deliberately shut their doors to Jews trying to escape the Nazi barbarity.

In some respects, Hitler won at least one of the two wars he began in 1939. He lost his war of conquest and German expansion, but he won the war against the Jews. He has been reported to have said that he will kill Europe's Jews and Germany will become richer and more powerful. Both of these predictions have come true. He murdered two-thirds of Europe's Jews, and following the war and the Marshall Plan, Germany has become the wealthiest and most powerful nation in Europe.

Would all this have happened if the Turkish government had been brought to justice for the genocide it committed against the Armenian people? We can never know the answer to that haunting question. But we can know that the world's reaction to genocides has been weak at best. Turkey paid little or no price for its mass murders. Nor did Germany.

In the case of Germany, a relatively small number of high-ranking Nazi officials were prosecuted and convicted. A few handfuls were executed. Many of those who were imprisoned were soon freed by the American high commissioner in Germany, an anti-Semite named John McCloy, who loved Germany as much as he hated Jews.

Following the disclosures of the Holocaust following World War II, the world pledged, "Never again." But since then, we have seen mass murders including genocides again and again and again and again. The international community condemns the perpetrators and sympathizes with the victims, but it does little or nothing to prevent these mass killings.

The Armenian genocide was not the first time in human history when mass murder was committed against an ethnic or religious group. The Chmielnicki massacres in 1648 not only were not condemned, but Chmielnicki was praised as a national hero. A statue of him remains near the center of Kyiv. More recently, several Ukrainian Nazi leaders who were directly complicit in the Holocaust have been honored by the Kyiv government.

Any tyrant now contemplating a future genocide will look back at this sordid history and conclude that the international community will do little or nothing to prevent or even punish those who commit such atrocities. The United Nations has devoted more time to condemning Israel for its carefully modulated defensive wars than it has to condemning unjustified mass killings in Africa and Asia.

Anyone who denies the Armenian genocide must be classified as deniers along with those who mendaciously deny the Holocaust. All genocide deniers raise the potential for future genocides.

Was Germany's Post-war Enrichment through the Marshall Plan Immoral?

The successful emergence of Germany from the horrors it inflicted during WWII cannot be denied. But neither should the moral costs of that success be denied.

The Marshall Plan, which rebuilt and enriched West Germany following the war helped it become the showcase of Western capitalism in the face of the Eastern communism of the Soviet Union and the countries it controlled, including East Germany. Part of the reason why the Berlin Wall came down and Russian Communism ended was the more affluent lives being lived by the citizens of those nations that were not under Soviet control. The Marshall Plan worked as it was intended to.

But what about the moral costs of enriching West Germany and its people so soon after the horrors of the Holocaust were fully documented at the Nuremberg trials and by historians? Hitler told the German people that if they got rid of the Jews, they would prosper. The Marshall Plan made that lethal prediction come true for West Germans (and for East Germans as well, following the unification).

Perhaps it was a moral cost worth incurring, especially in light of the positive outcome for democracy. But it was a significant, indeed incalculable, cost that has rarely been acknowledged.

The great German philosopher Immanuel Kant would have recognized the moral cost of rewarding Germany, and so many of its hands-on Nazi mass murderers, in order to achieve the important pragmatic goal of winning the Cold War. Kant famously argued that punishment for past serious crimes like murder must be deemed an end unto itself, not a means of achieving future benefits. To illustrate the absoluteness of this categoric imperative, he devised the following hypothetical: "Even if a civil society were to dissolve itself by common agreement, the last murderer remaining in prison must first be executed."

Most people would agree that this extreme example takes the principle too far. There must be room for compassion, rehabilitation, and important future considerations. But many would also agree that the imperative of punishing serious crimes must be given considerable weight in any moral calculus. Even those who would give it less weight should be troubled by any result that rewards, rather than punishes, past criminality in order to promote future goals. A balance must be struck between the moral imperative of punishing (and not rewarding) past crimes and the pragmatic needs of promoting future benefits, such as defeating totalitarianism.

The critical question, therefore, is whether the post-war response to Nazi atrocities—the Marshall Plan coupled with the trials of individual Nazi war criminals —struck the proper balance.

I think it did not. Too many Nazis and Nazi collaborators lived too good lives, unrepentant for their horrible crimes. Too few were punished or even condemned. Too many companies that worked slaves to their deaths were back in business too quickly and too profitably.

The so-called Morgenthau Plan, which would have denied Germany the resources to once again become an industrial power, was opposed by many as too harsh. Some thought it wasn't harsh enough. The aging President Roosevelt put it this way: "There are two schools of thought—those who would be altruistic in regard to the Germans, hoping by loving kindness to make them Christians again, and those who would adopt a much tougher attitude. Most decidedly, I belong to the latter school, for though I am not blood-thirsty, I want the Germans to know that this time at least, they have definitely lost the war."

After Roosevelt died, the tide shifted toward strengthening West Germany. Hence, the Marshall Plan that turned West Germany into one of the strongest economic and industrial powers in the world and enriched its citizens.

I recall a class I taught in the late 1960s that included several McCloy fellows who were honor students from German universities. (Ironically, John McCloy was America's high commissioner to occupied West Germany who pardoned many war criminals and returned assets to criminal companies.) I asked the students whether knowing everything they now know about Germany between 1933 and the late 1960s, would they have joined the Nazi party in 1933? Most said no. I then asked them to put aside moral considerations and do a simple cost-benefit calculation based only on pragmatic considerations. The students were split down the middle. I wonder how many citizens of West Germany would honestly admit that knowledge of the future Marshall Plan would have influenced their decision whether to vote for Hitler in1933. That may not be the best test of the morality of the Marshall Plan, but it is certainly relevant.

The issue of the Marshall Plan is merely an example—albeit a powerful one—of the larger philosophical question debated by Immanuel Kant, Jeremy Bentham, and their followers: how much weight to accord the moral imperatives of punishing past criminality and how much weight to accord the pragmatic claims of the future. These issues were front and center following the Rwandan genocide and South African apartheid. They are part and parcel of an even broader debate between the absolute moral imperatives of the Kantian schools that include Jesuit and other religious thinkers on the one hand, and the alleged moral relativism of the pragmatic utilitarian schools of Bentham, Mill, and Dewey, on the other. This debate is most consequential when it involves issues of life and death, as it surely does in the context of the Holocaust and "never again."

Quantifying Death and Life

<hr />

Death is different. And the rules governing death-and-life decisions should reflect the irreversibility of death. They should
require more certain evidence to impose the death penalty or to take
other actions that risk death.

Current US law does not adequately reflect the finality and per-
manence of death. For example, the legal criteria for convicting a
defendant of a capital crime are no greater than for a misdemeanor
carrying a relatively short prison term. Proof beyond a reasonable
doubt leaves open the possibility of false convictions. Even the rhe-
torical claim that "it is better that ten guilty persons escape than
that one innocent suffers" allows for some innocents to be convicted. Indeed, the historical origin of that famous quote was in the
context of the death penalty for which Maimonides required "absolute certainty," on the ground that it is better "to acquit a thousand guilty persons than to put a single innocent to death." Over the
centuries, the number was reduced to twenty by the British Judge
John Fortescue, and five by the British Jurist Matthew Hale, before
William Blackstone settled on ten. The same number was cited by
the Puritan clergyman Increase Mather, who said, "It were better
that ten suspected witches should escape than that one innocent
person should be condemned." Mather failed to apply this laudatory
principle during the notorious Salem Witch Trials.

The first recorded attempt to quantify the relationship between false positives and false negatives in the context of death was in the Book of Genesis, in which Abraham challenges God about his stated intention to kill all the sinners of Sodom:

> Will you really sweep away the innocent with the guilty?
> Perhaps there are fifty innocent within the city,
> Will you really sweep it away?
> Will you not spare the place because of the fifty innocents
> What are in its midst?
> Heaven forbid[1] for you to do a thing like this,
> To deal death to the innocent
> along with the guilty,
> That it should come about: like the innocent, like the guilty,
> Heaven forbid for you!
> The judge of all the earth—will he not do what is just?
> YHWH said:
> If I find in Sodom fifty innocent within the city,
> I will bear with the whole place for their sake.
> Avraham spoke up, and said:
> Now pray, I have ventured
> to speak to my Lord,
> And I am but earth and ashes:
> Perhaps of the fifty innocent, five will be lacking—will you
> Bring rain upon the whole city because of the five?
> He said:
> I will not bring ruin, if I find there forty-five.
> But he continued to speak to him and said:
> Perhaps there will be found there only forty!
> He said:
> I will not do it, for the sake of the forty.
> But he said:

---

1   In the original Hebrew, Abraham uses the word *Chalila*, which is closer to "cursed" or "blameworthy."

Pray let not my Lord be upset that I speak further:
Perhaps there will be found there only thirty!
He said:
I will not do it, if I find there thirty.
But he said:
Now pray, I have ventured to speak to my Lord:
Perhaps there will be found there only twenty!
He said:
I will not bring ruin, for the sake of the twenty.
But he said:
Pray that my Lord not be upset that I speak further just this
One time:
Perhaps there will be found there only ten!
He said:
I will not bring ruin, for the sake of the ten.
YHWH went, as soon as he had finished speaking to Avraham,
And Avraham returned to his place.

There is an obvious logical inconsistency in Abraham's argument. God could simply destroy the many guilty in the city and save the fifty righteous people. That would satisfy the premise of Abraham's rebuke about killing the righteous along with the wicked. But Abraham asks God to save the entire city—including the vast majority of wicked—for the sake of the fifty righteous. Illogical as it is, God goes along with this demand. This leads Abraham to engage in a typical lawyer's argument: Having convinced his adversary to accept the *principle*, Abraham nudges Him down the slippery slope. He asks God: What if there are only forty-five righteous people, would you destroy the whole city for the lack of five? Pretty clever. Then he asks the same question of forty, thirty, twenty, and ten. This argument is reminiscent of the quip attributed to George Bernard Shaw, who once asked a beautiful actress if she would sleep with him for a million pounds. When she said that of course she would sleep with him for a million pounds, Shaw replied, "Now that we've established the principle, we can haggle over the price."

God surely saw the flaw in Abraham's advocacy. He could have responded, "Look, Abraham. You accuse me of overgeneralizing—of sweeping along the righteous with the unrighteous. And you have a point. But you're guilty of the same thing: you are sweeping the wicked along with the righteous and giving them a free ride. If I find fifty—or forty or even ten—righteous, I will spare *them*. You've convinced me of *that*. But why should I spare the wicked just because there happen to be fifty righteous people in their city?"

Instead, God accepted Abraham's *moral* argument but eventually rejected its *empirical* underpinnings. God did not find a sufficient number of righteous people to spare the city, so He simply spared the handful of good people He did find. The important point is that God permitted Abraham to argue with Him on moral grounds, and although He eventually went through with the plan to destroy the city. He was persuaded by Abraham's moral argument. It was more than a Pyrrhic victory, since it established an enduring principle of justice.

The question remains, if Abraham's moral argument was illogical, why did God accept it? Permit me to offer the following interpretation, building on the idea of a God who is teaching as well as learning in His interactions with His human creations.

The text is clear as to why God decided to tell Abraham about His intentions in regard to Sodom and Gomorrah: because God had selected Abraham as His messenger to "instruct" his descendants "to keep the way of the Lord in order to do justice and righteousness." In other words, God's encounter was to be a lesson for Abraham in the ways of <u>human</u> justice and righteousness. An omniscient God is, of course, capable of distinguishing the guilty from the innocent (though He hasn't always acted on this distinction). Humans, however, cannot simply *discern* who are guilty and who innocent. We need a *process*—a legal *system*—to distinguish the innocent from the guilty. Nor is this a simple task. Inevitably human beings will make mistakes. We will sometimes convict the innocent and acquit the guilty. That is in the nature of any human fact-finding process.

It is easy to assure that no innocent will ever be convicted, if that is the *sole* object: simply acquit everyone about whom there is the slightest doubt as to their guilt, no matter how unreasonable. It is also easy to assure that no guilty person is ever acquitted, if that is the *only* goal: simply convict everyone against whom there is even the slightest suspicion of guilt, no matter how far-fetched. No system in history has ever managed to convict all of the guilty without also "sweeping along" some innocents. Every rule of evidence or procedure that makes it easier to acquit the innocent—for example, the "two witnesses" rule of the Bible—also makes it easier for some guilty people to escape justice. Likewise, every rule that makes it easier to convict the guilty—for example, recent reforms that no longer require "corroboration" of rape accusations—also makes it easier to convict some innocents. There is no free lunch or perfect system. The difficult task is to strike the proper balance.

In the end, every system of justice must decide which is worse: convicting some innocents or acquitting some guilty. Tyrannical regimes always opt for the former: it is far better that many innocents be convicted than that *any* guilty be acquitted. Most just regimes tend to opt for the latter: it is far better that some guilty go free than that innocents be wrongly convicted. This is the approach ultimately accepted in the Bible, with its generally rigorous safeguards for those accused of wrongdoing.

In addition to deciding on this basic preference, every system of justice must also quantify—at least implicitly. The Anglo-American system proclamation that has stated that "it is better that ten guilty persons escape than one innocent suffer" is surely an approximation, but it sends an important message: our preference for not convicting the innocent is a very strong one, but it is not absolute; we acknowledge that in order to convict large numbers of guilty, we will sometimes have to convict an innocent. We will try our best to prevent such an injustice, but we will not simply acquit everyone in order to avoid it. This is the way a mature and just system works.

Although it appears from the language of the narrative that Abraham is teaching God a moral lesson, it is also true that God is teaching Abraham a lesson about the inherent limitations on human justice, so that Abraham could instruct his descendants to do justice in a mature and balanced fashion—rejecting both extremes of acquitting everyone about whose guilt there is any doubt and convicting everyone against whom there is any suspicion. By accepting Abraham's moral principle—that a sufficient number of innocent people in a group requires the sparing of the entire group, including the guilty—God was teaching Abraham how to strike the appropriate balance. Since human beings are never capable of distinguishing precisely between the guilty and the innocent, it would be unjust to destroy a group that might contain as many as fifty innocents. The same would be true of forty-five, forty, thirty, twenty, and even ten. It would not be true of only one or two. It is significant that Abraham ends his argument at the number ten. Why did he not continue to try to bargain God down even further? After all, Abraham knew that there was at least *one* righteous person in Sodom—his own relative, Lot. Yet he stopped at ten, thus achieving a moral victory but losing the case. Why?

Here is my own interpretation. Ten, although an arbitrary number, suggests an approximate balance between convicting the innocent and acquitting the guilty. Without knowing the number of wicked people in Sodom, it is impossible, of course, to come up with a precise ratio. But the number ten, even standing alone, is neither trivial nor daunting. Since it is always possible that *any* substantial group of guilty people could include one or two innocents, selecting so low a number would make it impossible to construct a realistic system for convicting the guilty. But tolerating the conviction of as many as ten innocents would make any system of convicting the guilty unjust, or at least suspect. When the number of people on Illinois's death row who were freed because of their possible innocence recently reached double figures, the public began to express concern. Seemingly, the execution of one or two possibly innocent people was not sufficient to stimulate reconsideration of the death penalty, but once the number climbed beyond ten, even many death penalty advocates began to question whether the system was working fairly.

The Anglo-American ratio—better ten guilty go free than even one innocent be wrongly convicted—is also somewhat arbitrary, but it too uses the number ten in attempting to strike the proper balance.

What we see, perhaps, is an extraordinary example of interactive teaching and learning. God is willing to accept Abraham's rebuke—illogical as it may seem—in order to teach Abraham that he, a mere mortal, will need to construct a just and effective system for distinguishing between the innocent and the guilty. In the process, God too may have learned that He has been insufficiently sensitive to the plight of the innocent who are swept along with the guilty—as when he flooded the entire world, saving only Noah's family and animals.

The story of Abraham's argument with God has been particularly salient to me as a criminal defense lawyer. I know that most of my clients are guilty of the crimes with which they are charged. I know this not because they tell me—very few confess to their lawyers (only one has ever confessed to me). I know it as a statistical matter, since the vast majority of people charged with crime in America, and in other democratic countries, are guilty. Thank goodness for that! Imagine living in a country where the majority of people charged with crime were innocent. That might be the case in Russia, Iran, or China, but certainly not in any country with a relatively fair and nonrepressive legal system. So, I can safely assume that my clients are no different from the statistical norm—a majority of them are guilty. If anything, my appellate clients are *more* likely to be guilty than those of a typical trial lawyer, since my clients have already passed through the most significant check on prosecutorial error or abuse—the trial. They have already been found guilty by a jury. Some of my clients have been innocent, but they were almost certainly in the minority.

When I decide to take a case, I rarely know whether any particular client is among the guilty majority, the innocent minority, or somewhere in between. Were I to take the position—urged on me by many, including my mother—that I should represent only the innocent, I would probably have taken fewer than a handful of cases over my fifty-five-year career. It is extremely rare that I know for certain that a prospective client is innocent. I have my suspicions (which sometimes have turned out to be mistaken—both ways). I can never, however, be certain. This is even more true at the beginning of my representation, when I know relatively little about the case. As time passes and I learn more, I often reach a more informed view. Even if I come to believe that my client is guilty, I cannot leave a case once I have undertaken the responsibility for completing it (unless the client violates certain rules), any more than a surgeon could abandon a half-completed operation upon learning that his patient was sicker than originally assumed, or a priest could walk out of a confession upon being told of sins he did not anticipate.

I represent the probably guilty for several important reasons of principle. The first is that I, like all human beings, cannot always distinguish between the guilty and the innocent. If only those who were obviously innocent could get decent lawyers to represent them, many innocent clients would remain unrepresented by competent lawyers. I represent the probably guilty, therefore, in order to prevent injustice to the possibly innocent. This is in the tradition of the Sodom narrative, at least as I interpret it.

Second, I represent the probably guilty to assure that the government is always challenged, that it never gets sloppy, lazy, or corrupt. If our legal system were ever permitted to act on the statistical assumptions that the vast majority of defendants are guilty, then prosecutors would grow less careful about whom they charged with crime, and the statistics might become reversed, as it has in some autocratic regimes. Abraham understood how important it was to challenge authority, even divine authority. Although God was eventually able to carry out His plan against the sinners of Sodom, Abraham made it tougher for God. In the end, some of my clients have gone to prison—thankfully none have ever been executed—but I try hard to challenge the government at every turn. In doing so, I'm following in the tradition of advocacy originated by Abraham.

Third, I am a teacher, and I must teach by example. I cannot tell my students that *they* should represent defendants who may be guilty, but that *I* am too good for such dirty work. If our legal system requires that all defendants be represented by zealous lawyers, then I must be willing to serve in that role, no matter how personally unpleasant it may sometimes be. And believe me, it has been. Abraham, too, was a teacher, and he has taught generations of human rights advocates never to remain silent in the face of a perceived injustice—even if it means standing up for the guilty.

It is always distressing when the guilty go free. But it is a price we must be willing to pay for assuring that the innocent are only rarely convicted. The occasional acquittal of the guilty to preserve the rights of all is a difficult concept that continues to confound and engender controversy, but it lies at the core of any civilized concept of justice. In the Sodom narrative, we see God as a great teacher and Abraham as a challenging student. Both learn from the exchange. God learns that might alone does not make right, and that it is unjust to sweep the innocent along with the guilty. Abraham learns that right alone cannot save the wicked, and that perfect justice is too much to expect of any legal system. Both learn that the essence of justice is striking the right balance.

Nearly all death-and-life decisions since Sodom have involved attempts to qualify—sometimes explicitly, more often implicitly—appropriate ratios. Sometimes these ratios are between convicting the guilty and acquitting the innocent (proof beyond a reasonable doubt); arresting or searching the possibly guilty (probable cause); governmental intrusions on liberty such as deportation (clear and convincing evidence); or resolving civil disputes (preponderance of the evidence). Sometimes these ratios involve variations on the trolley problem (killing one to save five, four, three, or two). Other times they involve beneficial projects, such as tunnels, bridges, hospitals, high risers, and other structures, the construction of which probably will cause a certain number of deaths. In still other situations, such as wartime actions, decisions will have to be made as to whether a particular action—such as the atomic bombing of Hiroshima or the invasion of France on D-Day—will take or save more lives, and how to measure the anticipated cost in enemy lives, both civilian and military, in taking or not taking that action. A related decision is whether the action satisfied the legal requirement of "proportionality," which provides no numbers but demands that the expected civilian casualties be "proportional" to the expected military gains.

In each of these situations, and others, an appropriate balance must be struck, and the question recurs: in a democracy, <u>who</u> gets to strike that balance?

A lawyer friend of mine has spent most of his career trying to quantify death and life. His job has been to decide how much should be paid to the families of those killed and injured in human-caused disasters, such as the 9/11 terrorist attacks, Agent Orange, the BP Deepwater Horizon oil spill, airline crashes, and other such mass casualty events. It is a daunting task. There are charts and pictures illustrating what juries, judges, and other governmental agencies have decided about the worth of a life, limb, or function in workers' compensation and tort cases (arm: $153,221; big toe: $23,436; hand $144,940, etc.). Death is different. The loss of a life cannot really be measured by money, but in some contexts it <u>must</u>. Some economists have placed the arbitrary value at $10 million. But although all people are deemed to be <u>created</u> equal, their actual value, measured in economic terms, varies enormously by age, health, wealth, earning capacity, and other factors. My lawyer friend had to decide whether compensation should recognize these variables or treat every life the same. Would the trolley problem produce different moral outcomes if the one on the diverted track was "worth" more than the five on the straight track? Should organ recipients be placed higher or lower on the list depending on their economic worth?

The fact is—and this is an empirical, not a moral observation—that most societies put greater efforts into preserving the lives of their more "valuable" citizens than their "less" valuable ones. But that doesn't make it right. Again, the most important question in a democracy governed by the rule of law is: <u>who</u> gets to make these tragic choice decisions?

The brilliance of the Framers of our Constitution is that they allocated these death-or-life decisions among several institutions: state and federal; executive, legislative, and judicial; private and governmental; religious and secular.

In the end, the people govern through the power of the ballot. That is as it should be in a democracy, because death or life are the most important decisions of all.

CONTEMPLATING MY OWN DEATH

A Posthumous Letter to the Editor

—————

As I approach eighty-five, it is understandable that I am contemplating my own death. At this point in my life, when my statistical expiration date has already passed—a Jewish prayer recited during the High Holidays says that a person's lifespan is "three score and ten," and if fortunate, "four score"—I must be prepared for the inevitable. I am planning for my family to be well taken care of. Because I always like to have the last word, I am drafting this letter to the editor to be published after my death and following my obituaries.

A friend once advised me: "Never live for your obituary, because it will be as biased as the rest of media reports about you." Indeed, an obituary writer for the *Washington Post* called to tell me that my obituary would include the allegation that I had sex with Virginia Giuffre. He assured me it would include my denial. I told him that I did more than deny the false accusation—I disproved it! It will still be included, he assured me. That is why I am planning the following rebuttal:

Dear Editor,

I don't want you to think that I don't appreciate some of the kind words written about me in your obituary, but I had a policy throughout my life of setting the record straight with regard to things written about me, and I see no reason to allow my untimely death to change that. Your understandable emphasis on my high-profile cases and controversies distorts my record by downplaying the numerous low-profile and pro bono cases and causes in which I participated on behalf of obscure and indigent clients. I made it a policy throughout my life to devote at least half of my professional time to nonpaying cases and causes. I made enemies by defending unpopular and controversial defendants, such as Claus von Bulow, Patricia Hearst, O. J. Simpson, Leona Helmsley, Jeffrey Epstein, and Donald Trump. I am proud that I followed in the tradition of John Adams, who defended British soldiers accused of the Boston massacre.

Because of my representation of Epstein, I was falsely accused of having sex with a woman associated with him. Although I proved beyond a doubt—by her own emails and other documentation—that I never even met her (although her own lawyer admitted, "She was wrong, simply wrong," and although she and her lawyers ultimately withdrew all legal claims that I had sex with her), the false accusation remained in the public eye. The obituary writer for the *Washington Post* assured me it would be in my obituary, regardless of the facts. This despite her recent recognition that she may have "made a mistake in identifying" me as a person with whom she had sex. Thus, my need to set the record straight. That is the price of representing hated defendants like Epstein.

Among the causes I engaged in was the defense of Israel against unfair attacks. But I was not an uncritical advocate for the nation-state of the Jewish people. To the contrary, I was critical when criticism was warranted, as I have been regarding my own country. I supported Israel not despite my liberalism, but because of it—and because I have always defended just causes against unjust attacks.

I tried to live my life based on principles and consistency.[2] This was not always understood by those who disagreed with where my principles sometime took me and whom they led me to represent. That is why I have made it a policy to correct the record. Hence this posthumous letter to the editor, which I promise is my last word.

Sincerely,
Alan Dershowitz
(From where, I do not know!)

2　See Alan Dershowitz, *The Price of Principle: Why Integrity Is Worth the Consequences* (New York: Skyhorse, 2022).

Essay on God

It seems unusual to complete a book about life and death without reference to God—a subject about which I have thought, taught, and written a great deal without coming to any definitive conclusions. As I finished writing this book, I was asked to contribute to a volume of short essays—"elevator pitches"—proving God's existence. I asked if I could write one disproving the certainty of God's nonexistence. They agreed. Here is what I wrote:

If the existence of God could be proved empirically, then belief in God would be a matter of science, not faith or religion. But it is in the very nature of the concept of God that there can never be definitive proof or disproof of His existence. The case for God will always be somewhat uncertain.

The strongest case for God has always been a negative one: without a creator, certain observable phenomena seem unexplainable. The "God of the Gaps" explains what science cannot. But as science explains more and more, the gaps become smaller and so does the function of God. But there is one gap that will never be filled—that is inherently unfillable. Science will never be able to explain how something came of nothing. The Big Bang theory may explain how big (the universe) expanded from small (subatomic particles). But it cannot explain how small came from nothing. Similarly, evolution can explain how complex (humans) evolved from simple (one cell units). But it cannot explain how a living cell capable of evolving came from nothing.

It is this conundrum—creation!—that prevents me from being an atheist. It requires me, an honest skeptic of all things, to doubt the non-existence of God. It is not a traditional "leap of faith." It is closer to a rejection of non-faith—an enduring doubt about non-existence of a creator.

Maybe someday even this gap will be filled by science, though I deeply doubt it. I believe it is inherent in the limitation of the human mind to be incapable of imagining nothingness becoming something based on natural change. A medieval Jewish prayer (*Adon Olam*) characterizes God as having existed before everything (*b'terem kol*), and continuing to exist after everything else ends (*acharay kich'lot hakol*)—concepts that are difficult, if not impossible, for the human mind to contemplate. I recognize that earlier humans could not imagine many of the remarkable insights possessed by latter humans. But I think this is different!

The never-ending march of science may prove me wrong, as it has proved so many other skeptics wrong. I would welcome a natural explanation of creation from nothing, even as I strongly doubt its possibility. But until this gap of gaps is satisfactorily filled by science, I shall continue to doubt the nonexistence of God.

Does this qualify as an argument in favor of God? Or is it merely an argument against the certainty of His nonexistence by atheists who have no doubt? And does it really matter how one categorizes one's doubts about the existence or nonexistence of a creator?

My own doubts go back more than seventy years to when I was a troublemaking student in an Orthodox Jewish yeshiva. Every day we recited prayers that began *Baruch ata Adonai*—"blessed are you God." I composed a variation that reflected my skepticism and my struggle to overcome it:

"*Baruch ata* I don't know (or *adono*, as I pronounced it).
Baruch ata I deny.
Baruch ata I'm not sure.

Baruch ata show me why.
Baruch ata maybe so.
Baruch ata why not try.
Baruch ata still not sure."

The nature and quality of my doubts have varied over the past seventy years, but the constant in my life has always been skepticism about everything. That is my God-given right, gift, and curse.

Appendix A

MEMORANDUM TO JUSTICE GOLDBERG ON THE
CONSTITUTIONALITY OF THE DEATH PENALTY (1963)*

THIS MEMORANDUM IS ADDRESSED TO THE QUESTION, IS THE death penalty "cruel and unusual punishment, within the meaning of the Eighth Amendment?

CRUEL AND UNUSUAL PUNISHMENT

The proscription against cruel and unusual punishment first appeared in the English Bill of Rights of 1688,[1] was included in the Virginia Declaration of Rights of 1776, and was approved by Congress as part of the Eighth Amendment with little debate.

The first significant case to raise this issue was Wilkerson v. Utah (1878). The accused had been found guilty of "willful, malicious and premeditated murder," and sentenced to "be publicly shot until . . . dead." He did not object to the death penalty as such but, rather, to the mode of execution, claiming that it was not authorized by the governing statutes. The Court held that it was, and that shooting–a

---

* This memorandum was written when I was a twenty-four-year-old recent law school graduate. I have not corrected or updated it.

traditional method of executing certain types of offenders–was not cruel and unusual. In arriving at the latter conclusion, the Court made the following statement:

> Difficulty would attend the effort to define with exactness the extent of the constitutional provision which provides that cruel and unusual punishments shall not be inflicted; but it is safe to affirm that punishments of torture . . . and all others in the same line of unnecessary cruelty, are forbidden by that amendment.

Whereas *Wilkerson* involved a federal territory, the next significant case – *In Re Kemmler* (1890) challenged the power of a state to take the life of a murderer by electrocution. It was not contended, as the Court noted, "it could not be, that the Eighth Amendment was intended to apply to the states." But it was urged that the due process clause prohibited the states from imposing cruel and unusual punishment. The Court held that reversal would be proper only if the state "had committed an error so gross as to amount in law to a denial . . . of due process," and that the state's conclusion – based as it was on "a voluminous mass of evidence" – that electrocution was a most humane mode of execution was not such an error. The Court quoted the above-cited paragraph from *Wilkerson* and added the following dictum:

> Punishments are cure when they involve torture or a lingering death but the punishment of death is not cruel, within the meaning of that words as used it the Constitution. It implies there is something inhuman and barbarous, something more than the mere extinguishment of life.

Up to this time, therefore, the only alleged violations of the cruel and unusual punishment proscription involved not the extent of the punishment (i.e., death), but the mode of inflicting that assuredly valid punishment (i.e., shooting, electrocution). The next case, O'Neil v. Vermont (1892), raised the question of proportionality in the context of a long prison term and heavy fine and saw the Court divided over the meaning and application of the Eighth Amendment for the first time. A jury found O'Neil guilty of o307 separate offenses of illegally selling intoxicating liquor, under a statute that made each sale a separate offense. He was sentenced to pay an aggregate fine of $6,140, and if that fine were not paid within a designated period od time, "he should be confined at hard labor, in the house of correction ... for the term of 19,914 days." The Court declined to consider whether this punishment was cruel and unusual "because as a Federal question it is not assigned as error, not ever suggested in the brief . . ." and because, in any event, the Eighth Amendment does not apply to the states.

Justice Stephen Field dissented. He rejected the traditional reading of the Eighth Amendment, which would limit its application "to punishments which inflict torture," which "were at one time inflicted in England," and concluded that

> The inhibition is directed, not only against punishments of the character mentioned, but against all punishments which by their excessive length or severity are greatly disproportioned in the offense charged. The whole inhibition is against that which is excessive either in the bail required, or fine imposed, or punishment inflicted.

In the next case – which did not present the divisive question of the application of the Eighth Amendment to the states – saw the principles adumbrated in Justice Field's dissent adopted by the Court (by a vote of four to two, with three members not participating). In Weems v. United States (1910), an officer of "the United States government of the Philippine Islands" was convicted of falsifying a public document, and sentenced to fifteen years of "cadena temporal." This ominous sounding punishment was of Spanish origin and required the prisoner to "always carry a chain at the ankle, hanging from the wrists; [to] be employed at hard and painful labor, and[to] receive no assistance whatsoever from without the institution." In addition the prisoner was to suffer "civil interdiction," which denied him the rights of "parental authority, guardianship of person or property, participation in the family counsel marital authority, the administration of property, and the right to dispose of his own property by acts inter vivos." He was also subject to "surveillance" during his entire lifetime.

The severity of the penalty was not challenged in the lower courts, but the Court decided to consider it under the "plain error" rule, stating that it had "less reluctance to disregard prior examples in criminal cases than in civil cases, and less reluctance to act under [the plain error rule] when rights are asserted which are of such high character as to find expression and sanction in the Constitution or Bill or Rights."

After careful analysis of the historical experience, which formed the basis for the Eighth Amendment, the Court made the following observation:

> Legislation, both statutory and constitutional, is enacted, it is true, from an experience of evils, but its general language should not, therefore, be necessarily confined to the form that evil had theretofore taken. Time works changes, brins into existence new conditions and purposes. Therefore a principle to be vital must be capable of wider application than the mischief, which gave it birth. This is peculiarly true of constitutions. They are not ephemeral enactments, designed to meet passing occasions. They are, to use the words of Chief Justice Marshall, "designed to approach immorality as nearly as human institutions can approach it." The future is their care and provision of events good and bad tendencies of which no prophecy can be made. In the application of a constitution, therefore, our contemplation cannot be only of what has been but of what may be. Under any other rule a constitution would indeed be as easy of application as it would be deficient in efficacy and power. Its general principles would have little value and be converted by precedent into impotent and lifeless formulas. Rights declared in words might be lost in reality.

After analyzing the earlier authorities – including a 1689 case where the King's Bench struck down a 30,000 pound fine for assault as "excessive and exorbitant, against Magna Carta, the right of the subject and the law of the land" – the Court concluded that "the clause of the Constitution in the opinion of the learned commentators may be therefore progressive, and is not fastened to the obsolete but may acquire meaning as public opinion becomes enlightened by a humane justice.

In setting out the standards for applying the cruel and unusual punishment clause, the Court disclaimed the right to assert a judgment against that of the legislature o the expediency of the laws or the right to oppose the judicial power to the legislative power to define crimes and fix their punishment . . . [because] for the proper exercise of such power there must be a comprehension of all that the legislature did or could take into account, that is, a consideration of the mischief and the remedy. The states have a "wide range of power . . . to adapt its penal laws to conditions as they may exist and punish the crimes of men according to their forms and frequency."

The Court then examined the penalty in question against the evil sought to be mitigated, and construed the "sentence in this case a cruel and unusual." In doing this, the Court observed that "the state thereby suffers nothing and loses no power. The purpose of punishment is fulfilled, crime is repressed by penalties of just, not tormenting, severity, its petition is prevented, and hope is given for the reformation of the criminal." The Court concluded that since no legal sentence could be imposed under the governing law, "the judgment must be reversed, with directions to dismiss the proceedings."

Justice Edward White filed a dissenting opinion that was concurred in by Justice Oliver Wendell Holmes. The dissent accused the Court of considering the punishment in the abstract.

I say only abstractly considered, because the first impression produced by the merely abstract view of the subject is met by the admonition that the duty of defining and punishing crime has never in any civilized country been exerted upon mere abstract considerations of the inherent nature of the crime punished, but has always involved the most practical consideration of the tendency at a particular time to commit certain crimes, of the difficulty of repressing

154154

the same, and of how far it is necessary to impose stern remedies to prevent the commission of such crimes. And, of course, as these considerations involved the necessity for a familiarity with local conditions in the Philippine Islands which I do not possess, such want to knowledge at once additionally admonishes me of the wrong to arise from forming a judgment upon insufficient data or without a knowledge of the subject-matter upon which the judgment is to be exerted.

The dissent concluded that the proscription was intended as a limitation only upon the infliction of "unnecessary bodily suffering through a resort to inhuman methods."

Thus, the *Weems* case seems to be the turning point in the construction of the cruel and unusual punishment clause. To be sure, the earlier cases used words like *unnecessary* and *excessive*. But in those cases, the words were directed to the mode of effecting a punishment, the extent of which was not challenged. For example, on the assumption that death is a valid punishment for murder, the question was whether shooting produces *unnecessary* or *excessive* pain in causing death. The question posed and apparently answered in *Weems* was whether the extent of a given punishment was unnecessarily or excessively harsh, considering the admitted legislative power to "repress" crime, prevent its repetition , and reform the criminal.

In light of its antecedents, therefore, the Weems case can be read as announcing the following test: giving full weight to reasonable legislative findings, a punishment is cruel and unusual if a less severe one can as effectively achieve the permissible ends of punishment (i.e., deterrence, isolation, rehabilitation, or whatever the contemporary society considers the permissible ends of punishment). To this test must be of course added the traditional test: regardless of how effective they maybe in achieving the permissible ends of punishment, certain punishments are always cruel and unusual if they offend the contemporary sense of decency(e.g., torture) or if the evil they produce is disproportionally higher than the harm they seek to prevent (e.g., the death penalty for economic crimes).

These two tests are apparently recognized by the opinions com-promising he majority in *Trop v. Dulles*, when the Court in 1958 held unconstitutional a federal statute "punishing" desertion by expatri-ation. The chief justice, after reviewing the history of the Eighth Amendment and its application, concluded that the Amendment must draw its meaning from the evolving standards of decency that mark the progress of a maturing society." This seems to imply that no matter how effective certain penalties may be, they are uncon-stitutional if they offend such standards. Justice Brennan seems to have adopted the other test: "Clearly the severity of the penalty, in the case of a serious offense, is not enough to invalidate it where the nature of the penalty if rationally directed to achieve the legitimate ends of punishment." In addition to rehabilitation, Justice Brennan included deterrence and insulation of the offender among the per-missible purposes of punishment.

Justice William O. Douglas employed this test also, in his concur-rence in *Robinson v. California* (1962), when he said: "A prosecution for addiction with its resulting stigma and irreparable damage to the good name of the accused, cannot be justified as a means of protect-ing society, where a civil commitment would so as well" (emphasis added).

Tests for Cruel and Unusual Punishment
This section of the memorandum will attempt to apply the cruel and unusual punishment tests derived from the foregoing decisions.

1. If, regardless of its effectiveness in preventing, for example murder, it is condemned as inherently barbaric or uncivilized by "the evolving standards of decency" now prevalent in our society;
2. If assuming that deterrence, isolation, and rehabilitation[12] are the presently accepted goals of punishment, it can be con-vincingly shown that a punishment less severe than death can as effectively achieve these goals; and

3. If, assuming a consensus that life is more valuable than anything else, the death penalty is imposed for an act that does
   not endanger life.

The most that can be said about the present standard of decency
as related to the imposition of the death penalty for at least certain
types of murder is that it does not lean clearly in either direction.

There have been some public opinion polls conducted on this
subject (for what they are worth), and the results seem inconclusive.[13] The religious leaders of the country seem to favor abolition,
but they are by no means unanimous. The same may be said about
the commentators: the vast majority of writers favor abolition, some
professional prosecutors (and others of that ilk) have written against
abolition, and a very few thoughtful and respected writers have
opposed abolition (at least total abolition). Moreover, although the
worldwide trend favors abolition, there are still many civilized countries that employ capital punishment.

Against this background, I would agree with Justice Frankfurter
(concurring in *Francis v. Resweber*) that one is not denied due process when the state "treats him by a mode about which opinion is
fairly divided." If this is true, then the chief justice is correct in his
observation in *Trop v. Dulles* that the present standards of decency
are not yet sufficiently high to condemn capital punishment (for at
least certain crimes) on moral grounds alone.

The next question is whether capital punishment has any
uniquely deterrent effect on prospective murderers. It is generally
agreed among thoughtful commentators (particularly those of a utilitarian leaning) that if it could be shown that the death penalty really
does prevent murders, then capital punishment for murder is justified. For in that case, the state would not be "taking" a life; it would
merely be choosing to save one life at the cost of others. As Jerome
Michael and Herbert Wechsler have put it:

> We need not pause to reconsider the universal judgment that there
> is no social interest in preserving the lives of the aggressors at the

cost of their victims. Given the choice that must be made, the only defensible policy is one that will operate as a sanction against unlawful aggression.[14]

Or, as stated more recently:

The only conceivable moral ground which a state can have that will justify it in taking a citizen's life . . . is simply that one man's life is necessary and indispensable for the protection and preservation of many other citizens' lives.[15]

Thus, if capital punishment really does deter certain types of murder to a significant degree than any other punishment would, then there would arguably be no real objection to its imposition for those types of crimes. Capital punishment would not then be "excessive" in terms of at least one of the permissible goals of punishment – deterrence.

But does capital punishment really deter any murders? Much research has recently been conducted on this question, and many such claims have been predicated upon the results of this research. The most that can be said, however, is that "there is no clear evidence in any of the figures . . . that the abolition of capital punishment had led to an increase in the homicide rate, or that its reintroduction has led to a fall."[16] But as Professor H.L.A. Hart has warned, this conclusion (and the statistics upon which it is based) should be taken to mean only that "there is no evidence from the statistics that the death penalty is a superior deterrent to imprisonment"; it should not be taken to mean (as some have argued) that "there is evidence that the death penalty is not a superior deterrent to imprisonment."[17] Professors Francis Allen[18] and Richard Donnelly[19] have joined in this caveat. The meaningful question – at least at this point in the development of our methods of studying the relationship between punishments and crimes – is not whether capital punishment really deters crime (for we cannot know the answer to this question), it is "Where [does] the onus of proof [lie] in this matter of the death penalty?"[20] For if the state must prove that capital punishment has a unique deterrent impact, then it has failed. But if the advocates of abolition must prove that capital punishment lacks a unique deterrent impact, then they have failed.

This question assumes particular significance against the standard ordinarily applied by this Court in passing on the reasonableness of legislative findings based on conflicting evidence. The state is always presumed to act rationally, absent a persuasive showing to the contrary. This seems to suggest that unless it can be affirmatively shown that capital punishment does not uniquely deter murder, then at least certain types of murder may be constitutionally punished by the death penalty.

It may be argued, however, that the standard generally applied in passing on legislative findings is not applicable when human life is in the balance, and that to take life, the state must affirmatively show an overriding necessity. The Court has held on many occasions (admittedly in different contexts) that doubts should always be resolved against the application of the death sentence. See, for example, *Andres v. United States*.[21]

Putting aside the question whether the death penalty for murder is unconstitutional as a general principle, we may still ask whether, under the tests previously mentioned, the death penalty may be inflicted in a particular case or category of cases where it could not serve as a unique deterrent.

Consider, for example, the case of *White v. Washington*, presently before this Court on a petition for certiorari. In that case, the highest court of the state sanctioned the imposition of the death penalty on a murderer about whom the psychiatric evidence was unanimous that he could not possibly have been deterred by the threat of any penalty, no matter how severe, and about whom the court found that "there was substantial evidence from which the jury could have found that appellant could not control his own behavior."[22] It seems clear that for this type of murderer, capital punishment is not a unique deterrent; thus, under the test previously mentioned, the imposition of the death penalty on such a murderer would violate the constitutional proscription on cruel and usual punishments.

Consider also, the case of *Snider v. Cunningham*, now before this Court on a petition for a writ of certiorari (collaterally attacking his conviction and sentence on different but related issues). The district court, after a hearing on federal habeas corpus, found that the accused "has an irresistible sex urge which he is, at times, unable to control." And the Court of Appeals held that "he has little or no control of his sex urges in the presence of a female under his control in a secluded place."[23] Thus, it seems clear that although the accused may have had some control over the situations in which he might find himself, once he was alone with a female, the fear of capital punishment could not prevent an attempt to satisfy his "sex urge."

The foregoing case also raises the broader issue, whether capital punishment may ever be constitutionally imposed for a sexual crime that does not endanger life. A persuasive argument can be made – much more persuasive that can be made in relation to murder considered as a category – that the threat of capital punishment is not a unique deterrent to sexual crimes, considered as a category. Again, there is no convincing statistical data. But the psychiatric and psychological observations about the motivation of sexual offenses seem persuasive of the conclusion that if these crimes can be deterred at all, they can be deterred as well by the threat of a long prison sentence as by the threat of death.

Moreover, even assuming that sexual crimes not endangering life are uniquely deterred by the threat of death, there still remains the question posed by the last of the tests previously described: May human life constitutionally be taken by the state to protect a value other than human life? Certainly, if the value sought to be preserved were economic, the taking of human life would be unconstitutional regardless of the efficacy of the deterrent. Here, however, the value sought to be preserved is probably considered nearly as important as life by a substantial portion of the populace. Nonetheless, I would think that there is a general consensus that the value is still less than life. And when this consensus is coupled with the questionable efficacy of capital punishment as a unique deterrent to sexual crimes, a persuasive argument can be made that death may not constitutionally be imposed for sexual crimes that do not endanger human life.[24]

Thus, my tentative conclusions on the matter of capital punishment and the Eighth Amendment are as follows:

The Supreme Court should not at this time hold that the death penalty always violates the Constitution. It should hold that the death penalty for rape (and other sexual crimes) does violate the Constitution. It should hold that the death penalty is unconstitutional when imposed upon certain types of murderers (i.e., those for whom capital punishment is not a unique deterrent). It should hold that the death penalty is unconstitutional when imposed for certain types of murders (e.g., noncommercial passion killings about which it is fairly certain that capital punishment does not uniquely deter). It should carefully scrutinize the few (and becoming fewer) capital cases that come before it, in an effort to define categories of cases where the death penalty is unconstitutional.

In this way, as Professor Alexander Bickel suggests, "a process might [be] set in motion to whose culmination in an ultimate broader judgment [– the moral inadmissibility of capital punishment itself –] at once widely acceptable and morally elevating, we might [look] in the calculable future."[25]

Appendix B

A MATTER OF . . . DEATH

A nonfiction play[1] in three acts

The setting for Act I is a small law office in Atlanta, Georgia. The year is 1915. As the curtain opens, a lone guitarist sits on the court-house steps (which can be seen through the window of the law office). He sings "The Ballad of Mary Phagan." (This is a real ballad with lyrics and music written in 1915.)

Little Mary Phagan
She left her home one day;
She went to the pencil-factory
To see the big parade.

She left her home at eleven,
She kissed her mother good-by;
Not one time did the poor child think
That she was a-going to die.

---

1 The major events in this case are true; the names of the lawyers have been changed; and the dialogue—though based, in part, on actual writings and news accounts—is obviously extrapolated from the actual facts.

Leo Frank he met her
With a brutish heart, we know;
He smiled, and said, "Little Mary,
You won't go home no more."

Sneaked along behind her
Till she reached the metal-room;
He laughed, and said, "Little Mary,
You have met your fatal doom."

Down upon her knee
To Leo Frank she plead;
He had taken a stick from the trash-pile
And struck her across the head.

Tears flow down her rosy cheeks
While the blood flows down her back;
Remembering telling her mother
What time she would be back.

You killed little Mary Phagan,
It was on one holiday;
Called for old Jim Conley
To carry her body away.

He taken her to the basement,
She was bound both hand and feet;
Down in the basement
Little Mary she did sleep.

Newtley was the watchman
Who went to wind his key;
Down in the basement
Little Mary he did see.

Went in and called the officers
Whose names I do not know;
Come to the pencil-factory,
Said, "Newtley, you must go."

Taken him to the jail-house
They locked him in a cell;
Poor old innocent negro
Knew nothing for to tell.

Have a notion in my head,
When Frank he comes to die,
Stand examination
In a court-house in the sky.

Come, all you jolly people,
Wherever you may be,
Suppose Little Mary Phagan
Belonged to you or me.

Now little Mary's mother
She weeps and mourns all day,
Praying to meet little Mary
In a better world some day.

Now little Mary's in Heaven,
Leo Frank's in jail,
Waiting for the day to come
When he can tell his tale.

Frank will be astonished
When the angels come to say,
"You killed little Mary Phagan;
It was on one holiday."

Judge he passed the sentence,
Then he reared back;
If he hang Leo Frank,
It won't bring little Mary back.

Frank he's got little children,
And they will want for bread;
Look up at their papa's picture,
Say, "Now my papa's dead."

Judge he passed the sentence
He reared back in his chair;
He will hang Leo Frank,
And give the negro a year.

Next time he passed the sentence,
You bet, he passed it well;
Well, Solister H. M. [Dorsey]
Sent Leo Frank to hell.

As he finishes the song, the light fades from him and focuses on the two law partners. The senior partner is a forty-four-year-old southern gentleman named Brett Mason. Enormously respected by his peers, he is obviously a self-confident man with a bright future. His junior partner is a 28-year-old Jewish man named Benjamin Goldberg. Originally from New York, Goldberg recently had graduated from Harvard Law School and moved to Atlanta to make his fortune. His brashness covers an apparent uncomfortableness with the somewhat closed society into which he is attempting to break. The partners obviously like each other and thrive on their differences, which form a basis for frequent—if a bit self-conscious—humorous byplay. Mason dresses casually, in shirtsleeves. He blends comfortably into the background of the office, which is very proper but comfortably southern. Goldberg always wears a vest, a stiff collar, and a tie. He seems to be trying to break out of these rigidities, but at the same time wanting to be restrained by them. He is never quite comfortable, though he is always self-confident.

<u>Act I, Scene I</u>

Act I begins with Goldberg rushing into Mason's office, displaying a copy of *The Jeffersonian*, a newspaper published by Tom Watson—a popular southern race-baiter. The headline reads: "Jew Pervert must Hang."

Goldberg angrily denounces the southern justice system, which had recently found Leo Frank—a transplanted twenty-nine-year-old New York Jew who had opened a pencil factory in Atlanta—guilty of murdering Mary Phagan, a fourteen-year-old employee of his factory whose mutilated body was found in the basement of the factory. The dialogue brings out the basic facts of the case: that Leo Frank may have been framed; that Tom Watson's race-baiting fermented an atmosphere of antisemitism directed against Frank in particular and Jews in general; that Watson used the case to found the "Knights of Mary Phagan" (which eventually developed into the powerful Ku Klux Klan in the 1920s); that the Frank case—and its resulting defamation of Jews—created the immediate impetus for the establishment of the Anti-Defamation League of the B'nai B'rith; that Frank's conviction and death sentence created a furor throughout the country and the world; that Justice Oliver Wendell Holmes, Jr. wrote a stinging dissent when the US Supreme Court affirmed Frank's conviction and death sentence;[2] and that there was the constant looming threat that a lynch mob might get to Frank before the state's hangman did.

There is some discussion of the conflicting evidence in support of Frank's guilty and innocence, with Mason arguing (gently and tentatively) that there was enough evidence of guilt to support the jury's verdict, and with Goldberg arguing vehemently in support of Frank's innocence.

---

2 (Holmes's opinion ended with a statement that "it is our duty . . . to declare lynch law as little valid when practiced by a regularly drawn jury as when administered by one elected by a mob intend on death.")

The dialogue concludes with Mason suggesting that anti-Semitism was not a factor in the Frank verdict; that Jews have always
been welcome in Atlanta; and that it has been the involvement
of outside—northern—Jewish agitators and organizations that has
generated a tense and divisive religious conflict.[3] Goldberg disagrees
and lectures Mason—briefly—about the Dreyfus case in France and
other examples of anti-Jewish trials and pogroms. Mason is polite,
but unconvinced.

Act I, Scene II

Following this dialogue, Goldberg leaves the office for home and
Mason continues to work at his desk. There is a knock on the door,
and a shadowy figure enters the office. His back is always to the audience, which never sees his face. He speaks with a lower-class accent
that could either be that of an uneducated white or Black man. He
is a stranger to Mason, but he knows of Mason's reputation as an
excellent lawyer.

"I need you to be my lawyer. It's a matter of life and death."

Mason is cautious and makes no commitment. "I have a terrible
secret I've been hiding and I gotta tell someone," he continues, "but
there's no one I can trust."

Mason, becoming intrigued, assures his visitor that anything he
tells a lawyer he can be certain will be held in confidence.

The stranger isn't sure he understands: "You mean that if I tell
you about this thing, you can't ever tell no one?"

Mason assures him, in an almost routine way, that his secret
would be safe with him so long as it didn't involve a "future crime."

---

3   This is what one of the real lawyers, on whom Brett Mason's character is based,
     actually wrote:
         At the time of the murder there was little or no prejudice against the Jews in
         Atlanta. . . . The thing that did arouse a most phenomenal racial prejudice
         against not only Frank but all Jews was that just about the time the trial was to
         occur, various writers, speakers, civil rights societies, and Jewish organizations
         began to protest that Frank was being persecuted because he was a Jew. This
         whipped into flames . . . spreading racial and religious hatred.
     Arthur Powell, *I Can Go Home Again* (Chapel Hill: University of North Carolina
     Press, 1943), 287–88.

"What I did, I did," the stranger says, "I would never do nothing like that again. There was good reasons why I did it. I'm not guilty of no crimes. But I'm scared there gonna try to hang me for it. And I need your help. But I can't tell you nothing without you promising—I mean really promising—that you won't tell no-one. Cause no-one knows, 'cept me."

Mason again assures him: "Look, I took an oath—I swore to God—before I became a lawyer that whatever a client, or a prospective client, tells me in confidence goes no further than this office. I tell my partner, sometimes my wife who helps out around the office, but absolutely no-one else. You can count on it. If you want to tell me your secret, go ahead. If you don't want to, you don't have to."

"Will you take my case?" the stranger asks.

"I don't know," Mason replies. "That will depend on lots of things. I will consider it and discuss it with my partner and my wife."

"But what if you decide not to take it," the stranger asks, "will you still keep the secret?"

"Of course," replies Mason, "That's part of the rule. I will keep the secret whether I take your case or not."

"What if you telling my secret would help somebody else?" the stranger asks.

Mason responds: "That wouldn't matter. Once you've told me the secret, I owe my loyalty only to you, not to anyone else. You can absolutely count on your secret being safe with me."

At this point, the stranger begins to pace the floor nervously, fidgeting and crying. Suddenly he stops and says tearfully, "I trust you. I don't know why, but I trust you. And I'm gonna tell you."

Stranger: You know this dead girl Mary Phagan they're making such a fuss over. Well she was a no-good tramp.[4]

Mason: You mean the girl that Leo Frank was convicted of murdering.

---

4   The description of the victim is entirely fictional. There is no evidence that she was a "tramp."

Stranger:	Yeah, that one. She was a slut. I know her. She used to let me feel her, you know, breasts and things for a nickel. Now I'm real scared they're gonna think I murdered her.
Mason:	You have nothing to worry about. Leo Frank's been convicted of murdering Mary Phagan and soon he'll be executed.
Stranger:	But all them Jews are trying to get him off. What if he goes free and they start looking for who did it?
Mason:	What do you mean "for who did it"? Frank did it.
Stranger:	That's my terrible secret, Mr. Mason. I know that Leo Frank didn't kill Mary Phagan, because I was there.
Mason:	What do you mean you were there? What were you doing there?
Stanger:	We was in the cellar of the factory. No one was upstairs. I had just given that slut two nickels. Then she asked me for ten dollars, and told me that unless I paid her ten dollars every week, she would tell her mother that I had raped her. She said I would get lynched for raping her. I could never get no $10. I don' make that much in a month. I told her she wasn't getting no dollars from me, and she said she would scream. I tried to quite her down and she started to hit me. I put my hand over her mouth, and then she stopped beathing. I didn't mean to kill her, just quiet her. It was self-defense. My neck or hers. It wasn't murder. It was self-defense. I had to do it. But I didn't mean to kill her.
Mason:	Oh my God. You're telling me that you killed Mary Phagan and that Leo Frank is absolutely innocent?
Stranger:	He weren't even there at work during that time. He had already gone home. We never went down to the cellar when Mr. Frank was there.
Mason:	Well, what are you going to do?
Stranger:	What do you mean?

Mason:	An innocent man is about to be hanged for your crime. Are you going to let that happen?
Stranger:	It wasn't no crime. It was self-defense!
Mason:	Well if you think what you did was self-defense, why don't you admit it to the authorities and save Frank?
Stranger:	That's one of the things I came to ask you: could I plead self-defense if I killed her to save myself?

[Long Pause]

Mason:	I can't lie to you. God knows, I wish I could. I'd love to tell you that you could successfully argue self-defense or accident; then maybe you'd turn yourself in. But the truth is what you did was probably not self-defense or an accident. What you did was murder.
Stranger:	I ain't telling nobody, nothing. I'm not hangin' for no Jew. I want you to make sure they don't pin this on me, even if it means that Frank dies.

[Pause]

Mason:	I won't take your case unless you turn yourself in. If you let me reveal your secret, I'll do everything in my power to see that you get a fair trial, and I'll try to get a reduced sentence. But I can't promise anything.
Stranger:	I ain't turning myself in. And you ain't turning me in. Remember, you promised you would never tell nobody if I told you. Well, I told you. Now you gotta keep your promise.
Mason:	I don't know. You're asking me to let an innocent man die, by not revealing your secret. My God, how can I do that and live with myself? An innocent man's life is at stake.
Stranger:	My life's at stake, too. I never would've told you nothing unless you promised to keep my secret. Are you going to break your promise to save some Jew?

Act II

Act II is set in the gracious living room of the Mason home. The curtain opens on an already-begun discussion—really argument—among Mason, his wife, Amanda, and Goldberg. They all know the basic story that the stranger told Mason earlier that evening. It is after dinner, and they are sipping coffee. Mason is obviously perplexed and undecided. Mrs. Mason is gently but firmly urging her husband to save that poor innocent Jewish man. She is impatient with legal mumbo jumbo about confidentiality. She just can't understand how her husband could let an innocent man be hanged. Her words and actions suggest that she doesn't particularly like Jews and has nothing nice to say about Leo Frank as a person. But she insists that no one who is innocent should be hanged, regardless of any confidentiality.

Goldberg feels very strongly about Frank's innocence. Indeed, as a southern Jew of about the same age, he identifies with him somewhat. But surprisingly, he insists that Mason must keep the stranger's secret; that he cannot violate his oath, regardless of the consequences. He makes all the vigorous lawyers' arguments in a somewhat pedantic way typical of rigid young lawyers who know the rules but don't understand the need for flexibility. He repeatedly uses his own Jewishness and strong feelings about Frank's innocence to underline the importance of an absolute rule requiring nondisclosure of confidential information. For example: "Look, I'm a Jew. That could be my neck in that noose. If Frank is hanged, all of our necks will be closer to the noose. But I wouldn't divulge a client's secret even if every Jew in Atlanta were on death row and could be saved. Once you start breaking promises and turning on your clients, you might as well be back in the jungle where law isn't worth a damn. Jews need the law—even bad law—to protect them. We don't do very well in the jungle, where we are outnumbered by the snakes, jackals, and other slimy creatures who come out from under the rocks whenever a Jew is in trouble."

The discussion is heated. All the arguments in favor of and against disclosure are trotted out in contexts with which the audience can identify. The purpose will be to make the audience change sides—to be persuaded first by one point of view and then by the other. Finally, when the arguments have been exhausted—after about ten to fifteen minutes—Mason begins to look for a middle ground.

"There must be some way to save Leo Frank without turning in the stranger. Goldberg, stop arguing for a minute and start thinking. Use your wisdom, not your debater's skills. Don't make me have to choose between two wrong ways. Give me a right way. There has to be one."

The discussing then turns to various compromise approaches, which might result in Leo Frank's being freed without disclosing the name of the guilty murderer. Each suggestion has its share of problems. Act II ends with Mason saying:

> I think I've figured out a way to save Leo Frank's life without breaking any confidences. I'm not sure it will work. But it's worth a shot. I've got to do this alone. Have faith in me and pray to your different gods. I hope I don't ever have to choose between letting an innocent man hang and revealing the confidence of a client. I hope this will work.

Act III, Scene I

Act III takes place in Mason's law office. Goldberg rushes in with an "extra" edition of *The Jeffersonian* bearing the headline: "Jew-loving governor commutes death sentence of pervert." Goldberg is exuberant: "You did it, Bret. I don't know how you did it, but you did it. You saved Frank's life without turning in the killer. You really are a magician." Mason responds: "I'm no magician, and the sooner you understand that, the better a lawyer you'll make in this town. I used the most reliable and direct approach, the one that works best down here. I called the governor and spoke to him as one southern gentleman to another. I gave him my word that what I was about to tell him was God's truth. If he trusted me, as a gentleman, he had to believe it when I told him that I knew Leo Frank was innocent and that I knew who was guilty. I told him that no power on Earth could make me tell him who was guilty because that secret came to me through professional confidence. "I can't reveal my client's secrets, yet I can't live with them."[5] If he believed I was telling the truth, then he could not allow Leo Frank's execution to proceed. He pleaded with me for the name of a guilty person, saying that his job would be so much easier if he could point that finger at the real killer. But I told him that the killer's secret would have to go to the grave with me; that as a gentleman and as an attorney I had no choice but to keep the secret; and that as a gentleman and a governor he had no choice but to save Leo Frank from an unjust hanging. The governor sat there for a long time, and then he made the most moving statement I have ever heard. He said that "Two thousand years ago another governor washed his hands in a case and turned over a Jew to the mob. For two thousand years that governor's name has been accursed. If today, another Jew were lying in his grave because I had failed to do my duty, I would all through life find his blood on my hands and would consider myself an assassin through cowardice. I'm going to commute Leo Frank's sentence, because you have assured me that he is innocent even though you can't tell me who is guilty."

Goldberg: What does the commutation mean, does it mean that Leo Frank goes free?

Mason: Unfortunately, it doesn't—at least not now. All it means is that there will be no execution. Frank's death sentence was commuted to life imprisonment. We saved a life, but Frank will still have to stay in prison. Maybe someday his lawyers will be able to prove his innocence. But I won't help them, because that would reopen the investigation and expose my client to prosecution. Life's full of compromises, and this is one of them. I helped Leo Frank—but not enough. And I may have increased the risks to my client—but not too much. It was the best I could do.

Goldberg: You did the right thing. It was a masterful compromise, in the highest tradition of the law. You should be proud. We should celebrate.

---

5   This is an actual quote from one of the lawyers.

Mason: This isn't the time for celebration. I'm still worried about something.

Goldberg: What are you worried about? The execution has been canceled. The pressure is off. We have plenty of time to think about what else can be done. But right now, everything is on hold.

Mason: Not everything. Read below the headline in Watson's paper. He's threatening everybody: the governor, Leo Frank, the Atlanta Jewish Community. Everything may be on hold as far as the law is concerned, but the law doesn't control crowds. Mobs led by rabble rousers can take the law into their own hands.

Goldberg: But the governor commuted the sentence. Won't that satisfy the mob that Leo Frank was innocent?

Mason: The governor didn't say Frank was innocent. He couldn't. Because I refused to give him the name of the guilty person. If he had been able to disclose the real murderer, the mob would probably have been satisfied. But they may not be now. That's the real problem with my so-called "magic" solution. It really wasn't very magical at all. It poses some real risks of mob reaction. I hope and pray that the mob will pay more attention to the governor's actions than to that rabble-rouser Tom Watson's hate mongering.

Act III, Scene II

The last scene of Act III takes place at the window of the law office, as Mason and Goldberg watch with growing horror as the mob begins to gather and is addressed by Tom Watson. The outside action—with appropriate sound effects and perhaps silhouetted action—is narrated by Mason and Goldberg during the course of their heated and angry conversation. The lawyers describe the crowd: Mason recognizes two former Superior Court justices, an ex-sheriff, and a clergyman among the leaders of the lynch mob.[6] The mob breaks into the jail, carries out Leo Frank, and lynches him from a tree.

---

6   This is true. See Dinnerstein, L., *The Leo Frank Case* (New York: Columbia Univeristy Press, 1968), 139.

The play ends with Mason tearfully acknowledging that he had contributed to Leo Frank's death by refusing to face up to and make the hard choice between saving an innocent defendant and turning in his guilty client.

The End

As the curtain closes, the actual picture of Leo Frank's lynching is projected on the curtain, as the lone guitarist sings "The Ballad of Mary Phagan."

Postscript

Although the names of Frank's lynchers were well known, the coroner's jury concluded that Leo Frank died at the hands of "persons unknown." These same persons—the Knights of Mary Phagan— then established a new organization that took the name of the post-Civil War Night Riders: The Ku Klux Klan. The new Klan became a powerful force in Southern politics for a generation.

Brett Mason went to his grave without ever revealing who the real killer was. In 1982, an eyewitness—who had been a child stockboy at the Frank pencil factory—finally came forward and said that he had seen who the real killer was: an employee of the pencil company named Jim Conley. Nearly seventy years after his conviction and lynching, Leo Frank was finally cleared of all suspicion in the murder of Mary Phagan. Efforts are now underway to have the State of Georgia formally—though posthumously—pardon him and declare him innocent.[7]

---

7   In 1986, the board of pardons finally gave Frank a pardon, without "attempting to address the question of guilt or innocence . . ."